THE JOE BIDEN WAY

THE JOE BIDEN WAY

How to Become a Bold and Empathic Leader

JEFFREY A. KRAMES

AUTHOR OF *What the Best CEOs Know*

WILEY

Library of Congress Cataloging-in-Publication Data

Names: Krames, Jeffrey A., author.
Title: The Joe Biden way : how to become a bold and empathic leader / Jeffrey A. Krames.
Description: Hoboken, New Jersey : Wiley, [2022] | Includes index.
Identifiers: LCCN 2021028035 (print) | LCCN 2021028036 (ebook) | ISBN 9781119832355 (hardback) | ISBN 9781119832799 (adobe pdf) | ISBN 9781119833604 (epub)
Subjects: LCSH: Biden, Joseph R., Jr. | United States—Politics and government—2017- | Leadership—United States. | Presidents—United States.
Classification: LCC E916 .K73 2021 (print) | LCC E916 (ebook) | DDC 658.4/092—dc23
LC record available at https://lccn.loc.gov/2021028035
LC ebook record available at https://lccn.loc.gov/2021028036

COVER DESIGN: PAUL MCCARTHY
COVER IMAGE: © GETTY IMAGES NEWS | POOL | POOL

SKY10030059_101921

To Noah and Joshua,
whose shining souls light
my way forward every day.

Contents

Prologue: Lead with Empathy

Tell them what you really think, Joey. Let the chips fall where they may.

—Joe Biden's Grandfather Finnegan

Joe Biden landed in the White House with empathy on full display. The evening before his inauguration, President–Elect Joe Biden and Vice President–Elect Kamala Harris held a somber, thoughtful memorial to the 400,000 Americans killed by Covid-19. Biden acknowledged the unspeakably large sum of dead Americans. "To heal, we must remember. It's important to do that as a nation." He promised America that, if he were elected, he would make conquering Covid-19 and its ill effects on the economy his top priority.

A month into his administration, President Biden and Vice President Harris held another memorial, this time for the 500,000 who had died from the virus. Once again, Biden led with empathy: "We have to resist becoming numb to the sorrow." He asked Americans to avoid "viewing each life as a statistic, or a blur, or 'on the news.'" With feeling, he said we must "honor the dead, but equally important, care for the living, those that are left behind."

It felt like an odd but familiar moment and event. In celebrating and mourning the ungodly number of the Covid-dead, Joe Biden was playing a role played by other presidents in perilous moments: consoler-in-chief. He was better at the role than most presidents because few doubted Biden's authenticity. Even his greatest opponents liked and respected him.

The president-elect continued on that evening: "We often hear people described as ordinary Americans; there is no such thing. There is nothing ordinary about them. The people we lost are extraordinary. They spanned generations. Born in America, emigrated to America. But just like that so many of them took their final breath alone as Americans. . . . I know all too well what it's like . . . not to be there when it happens. I [also] know what it's like when you are there, holding their hands . . . and they slip away."[1]

Joe Biden's long-cultivated empathy was on display when he spoke of knowing about death. He had spent a lifetime remembering the deaths that so profoundly touched his life. The first tragedy was the loss of his first wife, Neilia, and their 13-month-old daughter, Amy, in a life-altering car crash in December 1972. Biden's two sons, Beau and Hunter, were also injured in the crash, but survived with serious injuries. A very shaken Joe Biden spent most every night with his two surviving sons, enduring a multi-hour, daily commute from Delaware to Washington, D.C., and back again. Far more recently, in 2016, Joe Biden lost his son Beau to brain cancer, the same disease that took his dear friend, war hero, senior senator, and former presidential contender John McCain.

His empathy as a leader has infused his storied career. Especially as president, Joe Biden has proven to be a likeable and reassuring figure, the importance of which was amplified

---

[1]Joe Biden, 500,000 Dead Memorial Speech, The White House, February 22, 2021.

because the Biden presidency followed one of the most chaotic administrations in recent memory. Even Republicans in Congress like the good-natured, avuncular Joe Biden. That has been true ever since he won his first Senate race at 29 years of age in 1972.

Early in his political career, a Democratic strategist named John Martella taught a young Senator Biden a lesson he never forgot: "You know, Senator," he said, "You should not run for president because tactically you can win. The questions you have to ask are why you are running for president and what you will do when you are president. You shouldn't run until you know the answers to those questions."[2] Joe Biden knew the answers to them. Being someone other than Donald Trump was not a good enough reason to be president. He had learned that a positive vision of the future is a politician's most essential driving force.

In fact, Biden's driving force has been to help level the playing field so that the impoverished and people of color get a fair shake. In words and deeds, Biden has demonstrated his penchant to help the Americans who had been left behind by the previous administration. As you will see, there is significant evidence of Joe Biden's earnestness in helping the neediest among us.

***

It is important to note one important point about this work from the outset: this is not a Trump-bashing book; nor is it an anti-Republican book.[3] This is a leadership book based on the actions and words of Joe Biden. Nonetheless, Donald Trump, the 45th president, and several of his allies are important to

---

[2]Joe Biden, *Promises to Keep*, Random House, 2007, p. 136.
[3]This author has voted for nominees from both major U.S. political parties.

this work for two key reasons. First, to accomplish his sweeping legislative agenda, Joe Biden needed Republican votes in Congress, and Donald Trump remained the de facto head of the GOP heading into the 2022 mid-term elections. Second and as important, the acrid political environment that existed in Biden's first months as president were, in large part, due to Trump, Trumpism, and the enablers who helped give sustenance to what were previously viewed as conspiracy theories.

Tell the Truth and Embrace Competence

Against the most unstable and troubled time in America since 1968, Biden found himself being named the victor on his third serious attempt at becoming America's chief executive. Within hours of the race being called, a seemingly rare commodity started to pour out of the new administration: *truth*.

The newly minted press secretary, Jen Psaki, gave her first daily briefing seven hours after the 2020 race was called for Biden. The new Biden briefings should have been regarded as unremarkable events, but given the absence of both probity and press briefings in the previous administration, they were a noteworthy and reassuring ritual for many Americans.

The other consistent commodity flowing from the new Biden administration was *competence*. When any member of the administration spoke, in briefings or television interviews, each looked calm, confident, and competent. There was one reason above all that ignited that confidence and enthusiasm: the fact that every member of the Biden administration knew if they upheld their integrity vows, their boss would have their backs.

Two examples of Biden's superlative cabinet picks were Antony Blinkin for secretary of state and Rochelle Walensky for director of the Centers for Disease Control (CDC) and the administrator of the Agency for Toxic Substances and Disease Registry. These two accomplished individuals epitomized the Joe Biden way. Blinkin served as America's 26th deputy national security advisor and America's 18th deputy secretary of state under President Obama. Walensky held degrees from Johns Hopkins University and the Harvard School of Public Health. Before Biden selected her for the CDC post, she was chief of the Division of Infectious Diseases at Massachusetts General Hospital while maintaining her post as a professor of medicine at Harvard Medical School.

From day one, Biden's cabinet stood in stark contrast to his Republican predecessor. For example, Trump's first choice for secretary of state was Rex Tillerson, who never worked a day in government (he was the CEO of Exxon when tapped for that key post). Tillerson, like many of his fellow cabinet members, did not last long in that administration (in fact, Trump experienced a head-spinning 85 percent turnover of his so-labeled A-team).

With a superb cabinet in place, Biden was able to focus on his key priorities. At the outset that meant mitigating the crushing health and financial effects of Covid-19. He became a better communicator, learning to strike just the right note with the American people. He learned to "level" with people while also transmitting a message of hopefulness. That form of messaging became Joe Biden's way of communicating with the American people.

Here is how Biden summed things up in the second month of his administration: "Today we are living through another long dark winter in our nation's history. Combatting the deadly virus, joblessness, hunger, racial injustice, violent extremism, hopelessness, and despair. But I know we'll get through this. Better days are ahead. I know it because I know the story of the journey of this nation."[4]

Embrace Diversity

At his first cabinet meeting a few months into his administration, Biden looked at the multiracial group he had selected and declared the following: this is a cabinet that "looks like America." Hiring a multiracial cabinet and team became Biden's calling card, his raison d'etre. His commitment to enlisting and empowering a diverse team to serve the nation—and not him—was one more Biden promise kept. Keeping promises, as the world was finding out, was of immense importance to the 46th president of the United States.

On his very first day in office, President Biden issued an executive order on "Advancing Racial Equity and Support for Underserved Communities Through the Federal Government." The order begins with Biden's true thoughts on the topic of diversity. We know he believes them because he repeated the sentiments often during his presidency: "Equal opportunity is the bedrock of American democracy, and our diversity is one of our country's greatest strengths. But for too many, the American Dream remains out of reach. Entrenched disparities in our laws and public policies, and in our public and private institutions, have often denied that equal opportunity to individuals and communities. Our country faces converging economic, health, and climate crises that have exposed and exacerbated inequities, while a historic

---

[4]Joe Biden, Remarks, The White House, February 15, 2021.

movement for justice has highlighted the unbearable human costs of systemic racism."

To reinforce his continued commitment to his diversity pledge, Biden signed another executive order in the early summer of 2021 "to advance diversity, equity, inclusion, and accessibility (DEIA) in the Federal workforce," he explained. "Enduring legacies of employment discrimination, systemic racism and gender inequality are still felt today," he emphasized once more.

"The federal government is at its best when drawing upon all parts of society, our greatest accomplishments are achieved when diverse perspectives are brought to bear to overcome our greatest challenges and all persons should receive equal treatment under the law," wrote Biden. "This order establishes that diversity, equity, inclusion and accessibility are priorities for my administration and benefit the entire federal government and the nation and establishes additional procedures to advance these priorities across the federal workforce."

There is only so much a president can do with executive orders. He cannot change the law, and even two executive orders are not close to a civil rights bill. However, in addition to policy they might change or improve, such bills set a tone that Joe Biden has no plan of taking women and people of color for granted.

The Biden Cabinet had the greatest percentage of women (almost 50 percent) leading cabinet-level departments in history. And half of the cabinet are Latinx, Black, Native American, or Asian American. Even America's first Black president did not have a cabinet as diverse as Biden's.

Of course, when it comes to diversity, candidate Joe Biden sent a strong message when selecting Kamala Harris in August 2020 as his running mate. Harris was not only capable; she was the first woman, the first Black American woman, and the first of Asian descent to occupy the critical office of the vice presidency. It meant the world to many black and brown women and children across the globe.

When Biden selected Harris, he was not only choosing a governing partner; he was also choosing a potential successor. According to management guru Peter Drucker, great emphasis must be placed on an executive's thoughtful selection of a successor. Biden understands there cannot be success without a strong successor ready to take over at a moment's notice.

Reach Out to Those Who Need You

Victims of Racial Strife

When Biden assumed office, racial strife had increased dramatically in the previous five years. White supremacists felt buoyed like at no other time in the past half-century. It felt, to many old enough to remember, like 1968. America was sliding backward in time as it pertained to the country's original sin. Biden understood this, addressed it in speeches and actions, and was resolute in leading in such a way that told Black and Brown communities that he at least understood their burden.

In the weeks leading to his inauguration, Biden understood that whatever painting he envisioned creating as the 46th president, his brush strokes would land on a canvas not of his making. He understood how badly his predecessor had marred the landscape and the violence it finally wrought. He knew he needed to heal wounds and that progress would begin with empathy.

Biden's empathy gene surfaced when, during the George Floyd murder trial in Minneapolis in 2021, he reached out to the Floyd family. He had previously visited the family in

2020, his first long-distance trip during the 2020 presidential campaign (he had traveled minimally because of Covid-19).

According to Floyd's brother, Biden wanted him and the rest of his family to know that people in high places cared about the murder of his brother under the weaponized boot of a Minneapolis police officer. Here is how Floyd's brother summed up the call with President Biden: "He knows how it is to lose a family member, and he knows the process of what we're going through. So, he was just letting us know that he was praying for us, hoping that everything will come out to be OK."[5]

Biden offered remarks from the Oval Office about that phone call and his feelings for the Floyd family: "I can only imagine the pressure and anxiety they are feeling, and so I waited until the jury was sequestered and I called. They are a good family, and they are calling for peace and tranquility no matter what that verdict is." Biden then said the evidence against Officer Derek Chauvin was "overwhelming" and that he "prayed the verdict is the right verdict."[6]

Biden wanted a guilty verdict because he felt it to be the just outcome, and the last things he wanted were riots erupting in cities like Minneapolis, Chicago, New York, Detroit, and Los Angeles. He did not give voice to that last thought, of course. But it was still a rare occasion that a sitting U.S. president commented on a case that was being tried in the courts. But this was no ordinary case—and no ordinary president.

Just a few hours later came the all-so-critical verdict: the police officer who murdered George Floyd was found guilty on all three counts. Justice had finally been served in the state of Minnesota.

---

[5]Philonise Floyd, Today Show, NBC News, April 20, 2021.
[6]Joe Biden, Remarks, The White House, April 19, 2021.

Joe Biden was heavily invested in the George Floyd murder and subsequent court case and its far-reaching implications. On the one-year anniversary of George Floyd's death, in unprecedented fashion, President Biden hosted the Floyd family in the White House.

Citizens in a World of Covid-19

When it came to Covid-19, President Donald Trump mismanaged the effort in spectacular fashion, by underplaying the threat, refusing to recommend or wear a mask, and lying hundreds of times about a pandemic he labeled as a "Democratic hoax."

A year into Covid-19, Anthony Fauci, director of the National Institute of Allergy and Infectious Diseases, was shocked by the extent of the suffering and stunned by the more than 500,000 dead Americans. The first year of the pandemic was horrific, "not only [for the] suffering . . . and deaths and loss of loved ones, but [for] what it [had] done to society and the economy, and how . . . [it had] deepened the divisiveness . . . making it more intense. People are going to be writing about this, and historically opining about this, for a long time to come."

President Biden was fiercely determined to get the virus under control and came out often to tell his fellow citizens to mask up and get vaccinated. The number of deaths decreased precipitously throughout Biden's first year in office. Within a few short months, Biden and his team were able to vaccinate three out of every four Americans over the age of sixty-five. That was a remarkable achievement.

The relatively high number of new cases that continued months into his administration only made Biden more determined to deal swiftly and decisively with Covid-19 and its dire consequences. He expressed optimism, but never stopped telling the truth to the people he promised to help.

Overcome Fear

Lies and quicksand have this in common: building anything meaningful upon either is futile.

Joe Biden entered office at one of the strangest, most perilous times in American history. A global pandemic, the threat of domestic terrorism, and a sinking economy were three great crises that he faced upon entering the presidency.

These unsettling events explained, in part, why unease ruled Washington in the first days of January, even before January 6. Instead of clearing and furthering a path for President-Elect Biden and his transition team, President Trump was focused on "stop the steal" and "the election is rigged" messages at public events and in speeches.

According to former Speaker of the House John Boehner, the problems with the Republican party could be traced back almost a decade: "By 2013 the chaos caucus [the Tea Party] in the House had built up their own power base thanks to fawning right-wing media and outrage-driven fundraising cash. And now they had a new head lunatic [Trump] leading the way."[7]

Most astounding, Trump never conceded or congratulated the leader who defeated him months earlier. He never acknowledged Biden's victory. Joe Biden sensed the coming havoc well before the election, when he declared to his biographer, "I am worried about them screwing with the election

---

[7]John Boehner, *On the House*, as reported on *Newsweek.com*, April 2, 2021.

outcome. When the hell have you heard a president say I'm not sure I'll accept the outcome?"[8]

As a result, fear flourished in the United States in the waning days of 2020 and the first days of 2021. That fear emanated directly *from* the Trump Oval Office, something unthinkable in the modern era. And that fear—which grew with each day— took two forms. The first: lawmakers feared for their jobs— their literal seats of power. The second: those same politicians also feared for their lives—and the lives of their families.

Cable news channels used the word *unprecedented* hundreds of times to describe Trump's norm-busting presidency, but never more than in his final months as president. It was then that Trump attempted to sell "the Big Lie."

The Big Lie was that Joe Biden did not win the 2020 election. Remarkably, Trump stated unequivocally that he, Trump, won the election "in a landslide." That consequential lie bled into the first year of Biden's administration and became a litmus test for all Republicans. Incredibly, total obedience to the former president became the only true North for members of the GOP, and senior Republican lawmakers proved that in just about every consequential vote.

Former Senator Al Franken of Minnesota summed it up like this: "We have two systems of information. And one of them is *disinformation*. Republicans in Congress seem to be terrified of the Trump people." Franken added that truth does not matter to the GOP: "It's a very, very, dangerous situation [that we are in now] in this country."[9]

The Big Lie persisted and had a chilling effect on the country. In late March 2021, the governor of Georgia, Brian Kemp, after his state lost the presidential election of 2020 plus

---

[8]Evan Osnos, *Joe Biden: The Life, the Run, and What Matters Now*, Scribner, 2020, p. 10.
[9]Al Franken, Interview, CNN, May 10, 2021.

the two Georgia Senate seats in 2021, signed a law making it more difficult for older voters and people of color to vote in 2022 and thereafter. The draconian law, as Biden pointed out, was antithetical to democracy. That did not stop other states like Arizona, Texas, and Florida from adopting their own vote-restricting laws.

The new Georgia law made it unlawful to give any voter in line water or food, even if they waited in line for many hours. The same law shortened hours to vote, reduced ballot boxes, and made it more difficult for all kinds of people to vote, especially the poor and voters of color.

That sent chills throughout the country and elicited anger and disgust from Joe Biden, who called it "an atrocity" and issued this statement: "This is Jim Crow in the 21st century. It must end. We have a moral and Constitutional obligation to act. I once again urge Congress . . . to make it easier for all eligible Americans to access the ballot box and prevent attacks on the sacred right to vote."[10]

One prominent lawmaker from Georgia, Congressman Hank Johnson, concluded this kind of law represented "a knee on the neck" of Black Americans.[11] The president of the NAACP in Atlanta, Richard Rose, said it felt more like 1921 than 2021.[12]

Raphael Warnock, one of the two Georgia senators to win his Georgia seat in January 2021, said that this issue was greater than any race or party or state: "Either we are a democracy or we're not," said Warnock emphatically. "This is a defining moment for the American democracy." Warnock then characterized the new anti-voting right laws popping up in states

---

[10]Joe Biden, Statement, The White House, March 26, 2021.
[11]Hank Johnson, Interview, *The Situation Room*, CNN, March 26, 2021.
[12]Richard Rose, Interview, *New Day*, CNN, March 27, 2021.

across the country as immoral power grabs designed to keep lawmakers in power: "Evil is well financed and determined," said the pastor and junior senator from Georgia.[13]

In the midst of these attacks against democracy and the fear they elicited, Joe Biden pushed forward to overcome that fear in an effort to restore voting rights to potentially disenfranchised people.

Understand Your Opponents' Intent

The late, celebrated chairman of General Electric, Jack Welch, lived by one management rule above all others: "Face reality." That was his first tenet of leadership, and it helped him to see things as they are and not how he wished them to be. He learned that from his mother.[14]

Joe Biden never worked in the echelons of corporate America, but he shared Welch's penchant for reality and pragmatism. And while he recognized that the Big Lie espoused by Trump was a persistent issue for millions of Americans, he knew the problem was deeper and even more embedded in the political fiber of the day. In 2021 Biden watched as hundreds of Republican lawmakers revealed their fealty to Trump over their oath to the United States constitution.

To succeed as the 46th president, Biden needed to understand what was required of him after four years of such a morally bereft predecessor. He also needed to understand the roots and ramifications of Trumpism and how that would play a role in helping him to secure needed Republican votes on key legislation. He needed to know how it could prevent him, Biden,

---

[13]Raphael Warnock, Interview, *The Rachel Maddow Show*, March 26, 2021.
[14]Full disclosure: I met Welch several times starting in 1992. I later wrote three and edited and contributed to four other books on his leadership techniques and models.

from keeping his promise to "unite the country," at least in the halls of Congress.

For historical perspective, Trumpism had an American precedent: the 1850s Know Nothing party. This party was anti-Catholic, anti-immigration, xenophobic, and racist in everything it advocated and represented. In summary, it was the "build-the-wall" party more than one hundred and sixty years before Trump.

When asked about what he thought of today's Republican party, George W. Bush described it as isolationist, protectionist, and to a certain extent nativist. "It's not exactly my vision," he stated unequivocally. Bush ran on a platform as a "compassionate conservative," which is a far cry from the party of Trump, which continued right into the Biden years.

Republican strategist Mathew Dowd helped to paint a portrait of reality when he set the record straight about Trumpism and the GOP: "The Republican Party created Donald Trump; Donald Trump didn't create the Republican party." In addition, according to Dowd, "Trump still enjoyed a ninety-percent favorability rating with the Republican electorate," even in exile in Mar-a-Lago months after Biden took office. In his discussion of the GOP, Dowd revealed the racist heartbeat of the Republican party: "What unites the base and Trump voters is not issues or points of view . . . [W]hat really unites them [Republican voters] is this complete hate of a diverse America . . . and America as it exists in the 21st century." Dowd added this bleak but honest conclusion: "The Republican Party did have a Civil War and the Confederacy won."[15]

Dowd concluded that it is something as noxious as racism that was the glue holding the Trump coalition together and in turn holding the Republican party together. Note that

[15]Kate Bolduan and Erin Burnett, Interview, *Outfront*, March 1, 2021; Matthew Dowd, Twitter, March 1, 2021.

this is not a Democrat or liberal leveling these claims of racism. Mathew Dowd has identified himself as an Independent since 2008. Just prior to that hc was the chief strategist for the Bush-Cheney Republican ticket of 2004. He was an old-school Republican.

Joe Biden understood the chaotic situation in the Republican party better than anyone. He commented often on the unfortunate reality of a dysfunctional GOP. "We need a Republican party that is principled and strong," declared Biden. "And I think you are going to see them go through this idea of what constitutes the Republican party."[16]

Fight Against Misinformation

Misinformation was rampant in America when Biden took office. In fact, well into 2021, the two parties in Congress and the electorate could not even agree on who legitimately won the U.S. 2020 presidential election. It was during this political seismic shift that Biden had to lead and legislate. If the rules of truth had changed, getting anything done would be a real challenge. This new reality posed an existential threat to American democracy. Aside from the time of McCarthyism, truth had not been weaponized in American politics to this degree since the Civil War.

Biden was required as president to battle this kind of misinformation directly and fiercely. After assuming the presidency, he was determined to bring as much probity and candor as possible to the American people, in particular by communicating often and clearly on cable and network news channels. He took a page from Ronald Reagan's playbook. Reagan

---

[16]President Elect Joe Biden, Remarks, January 9, 2021.

successfully took his messages directly to the American people, without the filter of the media or other politicians. This was Joe Biden's favorite way of communicating as well. All of Biden's speeches were picked up by two out of the three cable news channels (CNN and MSNBC), and the network evening news programs ran excerpts of his speeches.

Biden urged Americans to fight against misinformation and what he called an assault on democracy. "Look folks, here's the deal" became Biden's favorite catch-phrase. He would say those words while leaning over his lectern, lowering his voice, and delivering the facts plain and simple. Effective leaders do what Biden does on a consistent basis: they lean into the truth, they don't shy away from delivering bad news, and they do their best to convey as much information as possible to the people they serve.

Biden did not fall into the trap of hating Republicans because of their allegiance to Trump and the misinformation emanating from parts of the Republican party. From his first weeks in office, Biden was eager to meet with Republican lawmakers to see if there was any path, any compromise, for both parties to move forward on big solutions. Biden knew it was more complicated to govern an electorate in which a significant portion of the electorate and part of Congress do not believe you to be the legitimately elected leader of the country.

Unfortunately, misinformation grew and flourished in the United States during Biden's term, extending beyond questions about the election results to the Covid crisis, and it rankled him fiercely. "Misinformation is going to kill people." He was referring to misinformation about the vaccine which was causing many millions of Americans to go unvaccinated. "It's not a joke. . . [Not getting vaccinated] is like telling your four-year-old that when you see a red light, cross the street. I mean, come on," declared Biden with a tinge of anger.[17]

"What we are trying to do is use every avenue we can, public, private, government, non-government, to try to get the facts out [about Covid vaccines]," said Biden. Getting the facts out became a hallmark of the Biden administration.

Be Optimistic

No matter how bad the news, President Biden was always looking to a better future. He is the epitome of optimism. Biden often struck a hopeful chord in his speeches. That was especially true when he spoke of his deep-seated belief in the democratic way of life. When discussing America, he spoke realistically about how democracies could crumble. Biden emerged as the truth-teller-in-chief. He was a pragmatist, but he was also a lifelong believer in American institutions. A lifetime of experience in public life will do that to a politician, especially one as likeable and patriotic as Joe Biden.

In his inaugural address, Joe Biden started with a few words that sent a powerful message to friends and foes at home and abroad: "This is America's day. This is democracy's day. A day of history and hope. Of renewal and resolve. Through a crucible for the ages America has been tested a new and America has risen to the challenge. Today, we celebrate the triumph not of a candidate, but of a cause, the cause of democracy. The will of the people has been heard and the will of the people has been heeded. We have learned again that democracy is precious. Democracy is fragile. And at this hour, my friends, democracy has prevailed."

---

[17]Joe Biden, Town Hall, CNN, July 21, 2021.

Even in a speech that included a full picture of reality, Biden painted and promised a better future: "Our history has been a constant struggle between the American ideal that we are all created equal and the harsh, ugly reality that racism, nativism, fear, and demonization have long torn us apart. The battle is perennial. Victory is never assured. Through the Civil War, the Great Depression, World War, 9/11, through struggle, sacrifice, and setbacks, our 'better angels' have always prevailed. In each of these moments, enough of us came together to carry all of us forward."

What follows are the leadership lessons of the 46th president of the United States.

CHAPTER 1

Set One Priority

Successful presidents, better than me, have been successful in large part because they know how to time what they're doing. Order and decide on priorities.

—Joe Biden

In this chapter and later in the book, we will be invoking the work of great leadership thinkers like Peter Drucker (*The Effective Executive*), Malcolm Gladwell (*Outliers*), and Jim Collins (*Good to Great*) to help evaluate and put in context Joe Biden's actions as president. Drilling down, we will draw comparisons to see how closely Biden's leadership style adhered to certain tenets of leadership established by these thought leaders.

Focus on One Thing

The most prominent management thinker of the past century is Peter Drucker.[1] His many principles have stood the test of time. Drucker famously said that he did not know one effective executive who could focus on more than one priority at a time. Joe Biden knew this well.

Biden knew that he would be judged by how effectively he dealt with the Covid-19 pandemic. Biden knew that *he*, Biden, would judge himself even harsher on his response to

---

[1] I interviewed Drucker and spent time with him at his Claremont, California, home in 2003. He died two years later. My extensive session with him was his last known interview.

Covid-19. It is no wonder then that Biden's first reflex was to act, to do something, or to at least try to make things better for people. If there was ever a time in which that earnest form of presidential leadership was needed, it was when Biden took the oath of office in the middle of the pandemic, the likes of which the world had not experienced in a century.

In his first weeks and months in office, Biden's focus was unwavering. He understood the extent and complexity of dealing with the pandemic. He wrote, "Overcoming this pandemic must be our top priority as a nation. And while scientists have come through for us by developing safe and effective vaccines in record time, we need more than just a medical miracle to come out of this pandemic. We need to pull off a manufacturing and logistical miracle, too."[2]

With that one statement, Biden demonstrated that he knew more than his predecessor about what was needed to get the United States past the Covid-19 crisis. He knew which miracles were needed and in what order. He understood that to the extent he could control the agenda, he would have a good chance of success. But he knew better than most of his predecessors that life and events have a way of delivering some shocking reality when least expected.

The day Biden came into office, more than 400,000 American souls had already perished from the virus. (That number went up to 500,000 in his first weeks in office and continued past 600,000 in the summer of 2021, and 700,000 that fall.) He knew within days of winning the 2020 election that he would have to be a crisis manager.

The first test of the Biden administration was to get his Covid-19 relief bill passed through both chambers of Congress. Given the 50-50 Senate, there were zero guarantees.

---

[2]Joe Biden, Remarks, The White House, February 19, 2021.

And the stakes could not be higher. According to Pulitzer Prize–winning *Washington Post* columnist Eugene Robinson, gaining passage of the $1.9 trillion bill would be "the story of Biden's presidency."

Go Big and Keep Your Promises

It was with a growing sense of responsibility and ownership that the short-honeymooned, newly minted president made a vow to get Covid-19 aid to the American people. Throwing much of his political capital behind the bill—smartly labeled "The American Rescue Plan"—Biden was making a very large wager in his early days in office.

By any measure, this $1.9 trillion bill was a colossal relief package, the largest in history. As a point of reference, Obama's "American Recovery and Reinvestment Act," passed in 2009 in response to the Great Recession, was valued at well under half that figure. And yet Republicans railed against the plan in 2009 and repeated their name-calling a decade-and-a-half later. Never mind that under a Republican president Congress passed some hugely expensive relief bills.

How much aid money was allocated to help with Covid-19 before Biden came into office? About $4 trillion under the Trump administration.

In late January 2021, in Biden's first Oval Office meeting with lawmakers on either side of the aisle, ten Senate Republicans offered Biden an alternative package valued at just over $600 billion. The new president was underwhelmed—and soon voiced his objections to the GOP plan. That proposal did not come close to meeting Biden in the middle. It was less than a third of what Biden proposed.

After that meeting, Biden knew he and the Democrats would have to go it alone. Either way, he thought members of the GOP were thinking way too small. He learned from the 2008 Great Recession that he had to go big: "The choice couldn't be clearer," said Biden. "We have learned from past crises. The risk is not about doing too much; the risk is not doing enough."[3]

In that last statement we can see how Joe Biden had grown in recent years. He learned during the Great Recession that half measures do not yield great outcomes. And in every aspect of his domestic agenda, Biden was aiming for soaring results.

While the Covid-19 bill was still being debated, Biden decided to get right in the faces of GOP opponents of his plan. Here is how he threw down the gauntlet: "Some people say my plan is too big; that it cost $1.9 trillion. That it is too much. Let me ask them: what would they have me cut? What would they have me leave out? Should we not invest $20 billion to vaccinate the nation? Should we not invest $290 billion to extend unemployment insurance for the eleven million Americans so they could get by?"[4]

The stimulus checks alone, $1,400 for every American adult earning $75,000 or less, had a $400+ billion price tag all by themselves. Some economists, like Larry Summers and N. Gregory Mankiw, both concluded in respective opinion pieces that the total $1.9 trillion price tag was simply too large, that it risked overheating the economy. Mankiw, who served as chairman of the Council of Economic Advisers under President George W. Bush, smartly titled his piece "The Biden Economy Risks a Speeding Ticket."[5]

---

[3] Joe Biden, Remarks, The White House January 29, 2021.
[4] Joe Biden, Remarks, The White House February 20, 2021.
[5] N. Gregory Mankiw, *New York Times*, February 28, 2021.

While most economists sided with Biden's package, Summers pointed out that the bill could "set off inflationary pressures of a kind we have not seen in a generation." He also argued that the huge bill could siphon off vital government spending in other areas, like rebuilding America's infrastructure.

The Summers' *Washington Post* op-ed was concerning enough that it was read and passed around by staffers in the Biden White House before being publicly discounted. Some senior Biden aides felt that political calculus seeped into Summers' economic equation. The Biden team abhorred almost all the media coverage surrounding Summers' piece. Their disdain for it hinged, in part, on the fact that some in the press accused the Biden White House of "freaking out" over the op-ed.

All of this begs this question: Why should Joe Biden risk so much of his political currency right out of the gate? Why not go for something with a more reasonable price tag?

The answer is simple: He promised. Keeping promises is important to Joe Biden, an institutionalist born in the shadow cast by World War II. It is no accident that Biden titled his autobiography *Promises to Keep*.

It might seem a bit naive to believe any politician who insists he will keep all his promises. All politicos make such vows, and most break their word sooner rather than later. But Biden goes to great lengths to tell the American people when he cannot commit to something. The qualities of being straight and keeping his word were ingrained in Biden since he was a teenager. He remembers the trips he took to his "Grandpop" Finnegan and how his Grandpop wanted him to fully grasp two big truths.

The first truth entailed knowing that no one person or group is better than any other, especially when it comes to politics. You must "level with everybody," no matter what, regardless of which audience is going to like which message.

The second truth was that politics is a matter of personal honor. A man's word is his bond. If you give your word, you keep it.[6]

Biden was hell-bent on keeping his word even in the face of rising Covid uncertainty. In late February 2021, at a Pfizer vaccine manufacturing plant, Biden said that he thought America would return to a measure of normalcy by the end of his first year in office. But he quickly added: "I [may not be able to] keep that commitment to you. There are other strains of the virus. . . . Things can change. But we are doing everything that science indicated we should do, and people are stepping up to get everything done that has to be done." By late 2021, Biden was still hard at work trying to defeat the ever-changing virus.

Know Your Opponent Inside and Out

Every book that promises a potential heroic-like figure usually includes one or more people in high places rooting for that person to fail. This book is no exception.

Given the razor-thin majority in the 50-50 Senate, Biden knew that his greatest obstacle to turning his legislative wish list into reality was likely to be Mitch McConnell, the Senate minority leader (who had been the majority leader before the two Georgia run-off elections in early January 2021).

In the first months of the Biden administration, McConnell basically promised zero Republican votes to any major Democratic legislation. He did not want to give the opposing

---

[6]Biden, *Promises to Keep*, Random House, 2007, p. xv.

party a win. The policies did not matter to Mitch McConnell or to House minority leader Kevin McCarthy, whose political lives still focused on their previous leader, Donald Trump.

Biden knew how ruthlessly former Senate majority leader McConnell ruled the Senate for years (remember that Merrick Garland was nominated for the Supreme Court by President Barack Obama, and McConnell blocked a floor vote for ten months, until Trump came into office and nominated Neil Gorsuch).

McConnell, who served as the senior senator from Kentucky since 1985, stated unapologetically in 2010 that his chief goal was to make Barack Obama a one-term president. As Obama's vice president, Biden never forgot that.

However, in the final weeks of 2020 and early 2021 it was reported that Biden and McConnell had "been in frequent contact" since the November election. Friends or foes, the Joe Biden/Mitch McConnell relationship emerged as one of the most intriguing of the Biden administration.

Around the time of Biden's first press conference, McConnell evidently said that the two had not spoken since Biden had become president. But later McConnell walked that back and admitted the two had several conversations, ostensibly not about any substantive issues or policies.

It was more important to McConnell that people think he was behaving in a way to repulse the president rather than to get along with him. Things between the GOP and Democrats had gotten that bad.

McConnell also said he felt Biden had moved far left after becoming president. Biden was asking for six trillion dollars in his first three major bills, a triumvirate of unprecedented bills. He set out, according to some in the media, to outdo Franklin Roosevelt and the New Deal. His expansion of government was akin to Roosevelt's, even though the U.S.

economy was in far worse shape during the 1930s Depression than it was during Covid-19.

When asked directly about Mitch McConnell at Biden's first press conference, Biden said this with a sardonic grin: "Look, I know Mitch well. Mitch knows me well. I would expect Mitch to say exactly what he said." Biden added this: "I would like elected Republican support but what I know I have now is electoral support from Republican voters who agree with what I'm doing." Then Biden posed this question: "When was the last time a president invited the opposite party down at least half a dozen times to talk issues?"[7] In maintaining some relationship with McConnell, Biden may have reasoned: better the fox you know, than the one you don't.

Some political reporters pointed to McConnell's prowess in the Senate, citing different episodes when he outplayed Democrats. *Politico* ran a piece entitled "Enemies, a Love Story: Inside the 36-Year Biden and McConnell Relationship." In the piece, which ran two days after Biden's inauguration, the reporter cited McConnell as Biden's greatest hurdle in executing on his legislative agenda and getting anything done: "Between them [the Biden administration] and their agenda stands McConnell, an acknowledged master of Senate procedures, famed for his ability to block presidential agendas."[8]

McConnell certainly said nicer things about Biden than he did Obama (whom McConnell said he never trusted). And in 2015 McConnell was the only Republican senator to attend the funeral of Beau Biden, Joe's eldest son.

That did not alter the calculus. McConnell let it be known early on that he intended to live up to the more Machiavellian version of himself by blocking Biden at every turn. In a

---

[7]Joe Biden, Press Conference, The White House, March 25, 2021.

[8]Alex Thompson, "Enemies, a Love Story," *Politico*, January 22, 2021.

mid-February 2021 *Wall Street Journal* piece, McConnell stated unequivocally that he had zero desire to work with the Biden team.

McConnell seemed to enjoy the role of foil. He claimed that the way to "unify our [Republican] party" was to oppose the $1.9 trillion plan. He added this: "I don't think many Republicans are going to be for very many of the things that are coming out of this Administration."[9]

In March 2021, McConnell said this to a reporter who asked him about the bill: "This is a wildly expensive proposal, largely unrelated to the problem . . . so we'll be fighting this in every way that we can. It is my hope that at the end Senate Republicans will unanimously oppose it, just like House Republicans did."[10]

Consistent with a scorched-earth-minded approach, one Republican senator demanded that the entire 600-page bill be read out loud on the Senate floor. Perhaps in more "normal" times that sort of obstructionist posture may have seemed acceptable. However, in a post–January 6th, Covid-19 world, the posture seemed petty. Too many millions of Americans were hurting on so many levels, and Republicans in the Senate were doing everything they could to delay the medical and financial assistance provided by the package. Many members of the GOP were still lost, in denial, or comfortable with the oath-to-a-king taking place in their own party.

Work Through Intransigence

Since 2016, all that seemed to matter to the Republican party was one's complete and blind loyalty to Donald Trump. Saying

[9]Siobhan Hughes, "McConnell Doesn't Care about Trump Brand in 2022; He just Wants Electable Candidates," *Wall Street Journal*, February 15, 2021.
[10]Mitch McConnell, Remarks, Press Briefing, March 2, 2021.

no to everything—and everybody—Trump hated became standard operating procedure for Republicans, and like Trump, no one ever seemed to pay a price for intransigence.

However, in mid-February 2021, three weeks before the final floor votes for the $1.9 trillion plan, a memo circulated in the Biden White House. That two-page memo was authored by Mike Donilon, who advised more than fifteen governors and senators, as well as Vice President Al Gore, President Bill Clinton, and Joe Biden (in both the Obama and Biden administrations). The memo, entitled "The Cost of GOP Partisanship," detailed something of a reckoning for the Republican party. He also emphasized that the Republican party had a near-record-low approval rating of 30 percent.

Donilon then hammered the point home by comparing the approval numbers for McConnell and Biden: President Biden's were three times higher—at 62 percent!

Biden understood that while his friend/foe was just as cunning, he was not as powerful as he was months earlier when he was still majority leader. And that had to be going through McConnell's mind since losing the dual Georgia seats and, along with them, his majority leadership posting and a substantial percentage of his political power.

The year 2021 was turning out to be anything but McConnell's year. After losing his leadership position, he displayed the most serious kind of head-scratching acts when he acquitted Trump at his second impeachment trial and then immediately declared that Trump was completely at fault! He basically said that Trump should be charged with crimes and jailed if found guilty (it was Biden's Justice Department that would have to make that determination).

McConnell's speech on January 6 confused Biden and most everyone else. He had been one of the chief enablers of Trump and Trumpism for five years.

McConnell blamed Trump for losing him the Senate. He hated the former president. Biden knew that McConnell was fuming and that he, McConnell, would take out his anger on Biden, the new occupant of the White House. Within a few months, McConnell fell in line once again to serve the endless egomaniacal needs of the previous president.

In April, after Joe Biden presented his big, bold multi-trillion-dollar infrastructure plan, McConnell persisted with his stated goal of Republican intransigence: "That package that they are putting together now," said McConnell, "is not going to get support from our side. This is a bold left-wing administration, and I am going to fight him every step of the way. . . . I don't think they have a mandate for doing what they are doing."[11] He was fiercely determined to keep his entire caucus opposed to anything Democrats put forward.

And it wasn't just the Republicans that could help thwart Biden. The Democratic party had moved to the left since Biden was vice president and Trump was president.

According to John Boehner, there were troubling issues in the Democratic party: "What Nancy Pelosi and other sane Democrats—the ones who've been around long enough to know how things work—are dealing with from AOC and her Squad reminds me a lot of what I had to deal with during my days as Speaker from the far-right kooks of the Tea Party or the Freedom Caucus or whatever they were calling themselves," wrote Boehner.[12]

Still, even when Republicans fought him tooth and nail, Biden did not hesitate to push even harder to get his enormous American Rescue Package passed. In the days just prior to the House vote, it became apparent to Biden and everyone

---

[11]Mitch McConnell, Press Conference, Kentucky, April 1, 2021.
[12]John Boehner, *On the House*, St. Martin's Press, 2021.

else paying attention that the Democrats were on their own. No Republicans would cross over in a Trump-controlled GOP. That did not bother Biden much. He was disappointed, but what was about to happen was in line with his expectations.

He promised Covid-19 assistance and he knew that people did not care who voted for what. When thousands of dollars land in people's checking accounts, no one asks if the vote that delivered the money was bipartisan. They just want the money.

Biden, who was raised in a blue-collar, Christian home, understood the pain that permeated in the poorest of American families. He also recognized that it was people of color who suffered the most from the pandemic, for two reasons. First, it is always Black and Brown people who suffer the most when crisis hits the U.S. economy. And second, for some valid reasons, vaccine hesitancy was greatest among Black Americans in the United States (Republicans also ranked high in hesitancy). In 2021 just over 30 percent of African Americans said they would not get the vaccine, and an additional 20 percent say they were not sure if they would get it. This meant that half of the Black population had some version of vaccine opposition, at least in the early going (that would change over time).

Joe Biden was fiercely focused on overcoming all Americans' vaccine hesitancy. He emphasized the efficacy of the available U.S. vaccines at every turn, in statements, through his comms team, and on television. Then the administration and governors came up with incredibly innovative ideas to incentivize people to get the shot (e.g., million-dollar lottery tickets, using dating apps, etc.).

In mid-summer 2021, when the surging Delta variant became the dominant and most contagious variant of Covid-19 to date, Joe Biden decided that time was up for voluntary shots. He, and the country, hit a wall. And he decided to bring some tough love to the nation by ordering a vaccine mandate for all federal workers. Most healthcare workers cheered Biden's leadership.

Lead with Courage and Vision

Joe Biden was determined to get the American people along with Congress on board with his $1.9 trillion Covid-19 relief package. It was a defining piece of legislation, and Mitch McConnell and the old guard on both sides of the aisle knew it.

Two experts on the different forms of presidential leadership lauded Biden's approach. Gabriel Glickman, author of *The Rise and Fall of American History*, stated the following: "Joe Biden wants voters to trust him as a leader who will help restore America's moral compass. As Sen. Cory Booker, a former rival who has now endorsed Biden, termed it, . . . Biden is 'the best one to restore the soul of America. He is the best one to bring dignity back to that office.' This platform stands out today, in stark contrast to Sen. Elizabeth Warren's carefully laid plans and Sen. Bernie Sanders's plethora of policy statements, for not really articulating much of a substantive agenda. But Biden isn't running on policy; he's trying to gain the public's trust and restore Americans' faith in the political system—an aspect of his agenda from the very beginning of his Senate career."[13]

CNN's *GPS* anchor Fareed Zakaria also agreed with the president's audacious actions. He expressed admiration for Biden's leadership—for not watering down the legislation to appease Republicans. Zakaria wrote that Biden got off to a winning start with his domestic agenda: "Joe Biden has begun

---

[13]Gabriel Glickman, "Joe Biden's Big Vision for America," *Washington Post*, March 10, 2020.

his presidency with great success. He has moved to address the central issue facing the country—the pandemic—and proposed big, bold policies to help the country recover. He seems to have learned a key lesson from the Obama years: that Democrats do well when they act with imagination and courage, rather than waiting around and watering down proposals in the vain hope of Republican support."[14]

Zakaria also drew a comparison between Biden and Franklin Roosevelt: "The 1936 Rural Electrification Act brought electricity to rural areas. Biden proposes doing the same with high-speed internet which he argues is the equivalent in today's economy. Now the New Deal was bigger relative to the size of the economy at the time, but it is really the only valid comparison with what the Biden administration is proposing."[15]

One of the boldest leanings of Joe Biden is his "take-no-prisoners" style of legislating. Unlike other presidents who achieved great things, Biden had the slimmest of margins in Congress. And it was not only Republicans he had to worry about. Members of the Democratic caucus seemed to fight him tooth and nail on most everything.

Biden, a thirty-six-year veteran of the Senate, knew better than anyone of the forces aligned against any big pieces of legislation. That did not deter him, however, even when he knew his chances of success were against him. Throughout 2021, he pushed forward with multiple bills that would help the poor and lower and middle classes.

Adie Tomer, a senior fellow at Brookings, summed up Biden's boldness and vision after the keys to his infrastructure plan were revealed in early 2021: "What makes President

---

[14]Fareed Zakaria, Op-Ed, *Washington Post*, February 14, 2021.
[15]Fareed Zakaria, *GPS*, CNN, April 4, 2021.

Joe Biden's plan different? The scope and the spending are certainly bigger, far exceeding the Trump plan or anything the Obama, George W. Bush, or Clinton administrations ever formally proposed. . . . But perhaps something far more fundamental has captured the country's collective imagination. The Biden proposal is a philosophical statement of purpose. It visualizes a more inclusive, sustainable, and competitive country—and then offers ideas on how to build it. After four years of cynicism and abdication, the American Jobs Plan is a beacon of candor and optimism."[16]

Watch All Flanks and Don't Get Distracted

For months into his administration, it was obvious that Biden was content to let the Republicans fight among themselves. He wanted nothing to do with a GOP that continued to stand for intransigence and the man in Mar-a-Lago. He had more than his fill of the Big Lie, Trumpism, election-deniers— Biden had enough of all of that. He faced several crises and had a packed and pressing legislative agenda; he refused to be distracted by the infighting on the other side. And Joe Biden did not advocate holding grudges.

When reporters—or citizens at a town hall event—pressed Biden for a comment about his predecessor or the lack of spine displayed by Republicans at Trump's second impeachment trial and verdict, Biden did not take the bait: "For four years, all that's been in the news is Trump. For the next

[16]Adie Tomer, "Biden's Infrastructure Plan Replaces Federal Cynicism with a Sweeping Vision," *Brookings*, April 9, 2021.

four years I want to make sure that all there is in the news is the American people. I'm tired of talking about Trump."[17]

That statement was a master stroke. When given the chance to slam a twice-impeached president, Biden deftly side-stepped the question. He had too much class to get in the mud with his predecessor. Instead, he made it about the American people instead of himself.

However, Biden had to watch several flanks simultaneously. As a political animal whose tusks had matured in the Senate, Joe Biden developed the ability to understand equally well the contours and extremes of his own party.

On his left was the nearly 100-person Progressive caucus in the House. Members like Bernie Sanders and Alexandria Ocasio-Cortez wanted a more aggressive stance against things like student loan debt than Biden was prepared to take. For example, Sanders, Cortez, and the chair of the Progressive caucus, Pramila Jayapal, argued to have $50,000 wiped off all Americans' student loan debt. Biden was only prepared to go to $10,000.

To Biden's right flank were the so-labeled moderates, Senators Joe Manchin of West Virginia and Kristen Sinema of Arizona, who would pose their own brand of threat to Biden.

Every flank of every party has its own ideology and core values and issues. A few key issues became hot button topics among lawmakers of all stripes during the Biden administration. One such issue—which was under intense discussion and debate on the left and the right for years— was the minimum wage. The Democrats wanted a stepped-up $15 minimum wage. When Biden assumed office, the minimum wage stood at $7.25.

---

[17]Joe Biden, Town Hall, CNN, February 16, 2021.

As specified in the American Rescue Plan, the $15 minimum wage would not go into effect until 2025 (it would go from $7.25 to $9.50 immediately, then move upward each year until 2025). Progressive Democrats had a logical argument for lifting the lowest wages. There had been no increase in the minimum wage since 2009.[18]

Most Republican lawmakers abhorred the idea of raising the wage that aggressively—along with the two moderate Democrats, Manchin and Sinema. As for Biden, he predicted, and was confident, that the minimum wage provision would not make it to the final version of the bill (because of arcane Senate rules). That did not stop the minimum wage debate from raging on in the first months of Biden's presidency.

Pramila Jayapal insisted that the wage hike was an absolute necessity in the bill: "This fifteen-dollar minimum wage [increase] would mean thirty million Americans would get a raise," she insisted, adding that "a million Americans would come out of poverty, and thirty percent of those minimum wage Americans are Black, twenty-five percent are Latinx."[19]

It was in that space of reality—between the progressive part of his own party to moderate Democrats to an intransigent GOP—that Biden came to understand the difficulty of getting any meaningful legislation passed given his very narrow margins in both chambers of Congress.

Still, he remained undeterred and fiercely determined to get some important things done. Biden was the glass-half-full president who had big plans for the nation he served and now led. He was resolute in not permitting fiefdoms or flanks

---

[18]That stood in sharp contrast to Americans affluent enough to have a stock portfolio or a 401k plan. The value of stocks is up about 500 percent over the lows of the U.S. stock market of 2009.

[19]Dana Bash, *State of the Union*, CNN, February 21, 2021.

control his agenda, which he regarded as the people's agenda. Most every bill proposed by Biden in his first year had a plurality of support among the electorate. That meant he was winning over some hearts and minds among the Republican electorate.

In speaking in the small township of Lower Macungie in Pennsylvania in the summer of 2021, Biden showed two sides of himself that he has described to several audiences throughout the nation. "When I announced my campaign, and not many people took it seriously, I said I was running to restore the soul of this country with a sense of decency and honor; and secondly, to rebuild the backbone of the country. For hard-working middle-class folks."[20] In those few sentences, Biden revealed a good deal about himself: He showed that he is humble, that he is old-school in the best of ways, and that he would never forget the people who helped him achieve his life-long ambition of becoming president.

Communicate Directly

While Joe Biden's huge American Rescue Plan bill was being debated, he set out to sell the plan in his first town hall meeting in February 2021 with Wisconsin voters. A town hall event is the kind of venue that Biden loved but had been unable to host for a year due to the pandemic. Bypassing Congress to talk directly to the American people would become a frequent Biden tactic.

When given the chance to sell his plan, the empathetic Biden was more concerned with calming the nerves of an anxious electorate than he was in advancing his own legislative

---

[20]Joe Biden, Speech, Lower Macungie Township, Pennsylvania, July 28, 2021.

agenda. For example, when a second grader expressed fear of Covid-19 killing her, it was the classic Biden on display: "Don't be scared, you're going to be fine," Biden told the girl. "We'll make sure mommy is fine, too."[21] Biden also asked two other individuals to stay after the event so he could help them personally with their problems. (Biden did in fact meet with those folks in private following the event.)

It wasn't until about a third into the meeting that Biden turned to his legislative agenda, when he proclaimed the following: "It is estimated that if we pass this bill . . . we will create seven million more jobs this year. . . . You have ten million people unemployed—we need unemployment insurance."[22] But he did not hit Wisconsin voters over the head with his signature legislation. He figured Americans were paying attention, and he did not want to appear to be twisting arms at such a sensitive time due to the pandemic.

That "softer-sell" approach was emblematic of an empathetic leader like Joe Biden. He knew he did not like to be lectured to—and he treated people the way he wanted to be treated. His golden-rule indoctrination from his Catholic faith and upbringing played significant roles in shaping the way he led the country.

While debate over the package raged on, the GOP was continuing to fight Biden to help defeat the bill. At first, the best Republican lawmakers could do was to attempt to besmirch the package by calling it a "payout to progressives" and "left of Lenin." After that, they tried using more prominent voices in the GOP.

One such prominent Republican voice belonged to Ohio Senator Rob Portman, who wrote the following in a *Washington*

---

[21]Joe Biden, Town Hall, CNN, February 16, 2021.
[22]Ibid.

Post opinion piece that ran three days before the House vote: "Our country seems more divided along partisan lines than at any time I can remember. That's why I was pleased to hear President Biden encourage bipartisanship in his inaugural address. I agree with his statement that, at 'our historic moment of crisis and challenge . . . unity is the path forward.' Unfortunately, that rhetoric has not yet been matched by action."[23]

"Most disappointing," continued Portman, "is the partisan approach the new administration is taking to the Covid-19 pandemic, one of the few areas where there has been real bipartisanship over the past year. We know Covid-19 policy can be bipartisan, because Congress already passed five laws appropriating more than $4 trillion with huge bipartisan majorities."[24]

Republicans opted to use the only tool Biden had provided them—his, Biden's, own words. He had campaigned on a spirit and promise of unity and bipartisanship. He echoed that in his inaugural address: "[T]he answer is not to turn inward, to retreat into competing factions. . . . We must end this uncivil war that pits red against blue, rural versus urban, conservative versus liberal. We can do this if we open our souls instead of hardening our hearts."

Biden knew that, regardless of the united GOP front assembled against him, there were different slices of the Republican party, and some Republicans secretly favored the package. While different polls yielded different results, the mammoth bill was popular in the United States. The variance in polls was due to how questions were asked of respondents.

---

[23]Rob Portman, Op-Ed, *Washington Post*, February 23, 2021.
[24]Ibid.

For example, a CBS poll conducted by YouGov asked this: "Would you approve or disapprove of Congress passing an additional economic relief package that would provide funds to people and businesses impacted by the coronavirus outbreak?" In response, 70 percent of Republicans said they approved, while 95 percent of Democrats approved.[25]

Once the complete Biden-stimulus package was described in depth, with the $1.9 trillion price tag, the numbers changed, but only slightly. According to a Politico-Morning Consult poll, the week of the House vote, 90 percent of Democrats favored the plan while 60 percent of Republicans backed it, along with 70 percent of Independents.

Biden had both economics and history on his side. He also had the backing of Americans behind him. But there was often a disconnect between the reality of Main Street and what played out in the halls of Congress and the decisions made by the people's elected representatives. Biden's best chance of getting what he wanted was not only to persuade Congress itself but to communicate directly to the American people and hope that those representatives were listening.

What's the Takeaway?

- **Always Know Your Number-One Priority.** When Peter Drucker said he never knew a CEO who could handle more than one priority at a time, he knew he was being a bit simplistic. But Drucker was making a point, a point that Joe Biden well understood. Leaders following the Joe Biden way must not allow their agenda to be disassembled

---

[25]Amy Sherman, "Do a Majority of Republicans Support Biden's $1.9 Trillion American Rescue Plan?" *Politifact*, February 22, 2021.

or otherwise blocked by different factions of their organization. Each day they should know their chief "to do" item, and they should know what that is ahead of time by being prepared.

- **Level with Everyone.** When Biden's grandfather taught young Joe to be honest with everyone and "let the chips fall where they may," his message stayed with Joe throughout his life. Leaders may be constrained by how much information they can impart, but when conveying information to different constituencies, they need to connect the truth through every rendition. An authentic leader should never be caught in a lie. That is not leadership; that is risking one's reputation—something to be avoided at all costs.

- **Understand the Behavioral and Aspirational Aspects of Your Leadership Team.** Large organizations are made up of different types of leaders. In government, the diversity is even greater. Biden understood the importance of a great team. Like cabinet heads, business managers have different needs. Leaders at any level of government or business must educate themselves on the motivations and styles of work of each key individual who reports to them. They must not forget about the people who are closest to their constituents or customers.

CHAPTER 2

Execute Strategically

If we act now, decisively, quickly, and boldly, we can finally get ahead of this virus; we can finally get our economy moving again.

—Joe Biden

Before either chamber of Congress voted on the $1.9 trillion Covid-19 relief bill, Biden knew that his two biggest hurdles involved two senators—Joe Manchin and Kyrsten Sinema. He and everyone else knew they had problems with certain parts of the package.

Biden also knew that if the minimum wage provision were not removed from the bill in the Senate version, it could likely sink the entire bill. The minimum wage provision was one of the main attractions of the relief package for Democrats, particularly those nearly one hundred progressives who made up the left flank of the party. (Since the dawn of time, the minimum wage has been a divisive issue for every faction of both major political parties.)

This time, there were both Democratic and Republican lawmakers who felt strongly that the minimum wage provision did not belong in a Covid-19 relief bill—that it should have been in a separate piece of legislation. In fact, in the weeks leading up to the House vote on the plan, Biden signaled—no, stated outright—that he did not believe that the wage provision would make it to the final bill. He believed in the wage hike, but he was a realist and pragmatist. He was also evolving in his role as president.

One of the real advantages of being in political life for five decades was that Biden was afforded the long view of things.

He was playing the long game, although he was doing it in short order. Once he felt the momentum leaning his way, he worked with his leadership team, especially Senate Majority Leader Chuck Schumer, to ensure that the bill made it across the finish line.

Play "Three-Dimensional Chess"

During Donald Trump's term as president, cable news channel anchors wondered out loud if Trump were playing "three-dimensional chess" in his planning and plotting and tweeting. They concluded he was not, but perhaps Biden was.

Every move made by Biden to advance his historic relief bill was strategic in nature or at least tactical in practice, meaning that any course of action he pursued would have to be in service of his overall strategy. From courting Manchin and Sinema early on, to inviting Republican lawmakers to the White House, most of what played out was anticipated and planned for by Biden himself. If anyone was playing three-dimensional chess, it was Biden.

Biden knew that the path to getting all fifty *Democratic* votes in the Senate went *through* the Republican party; the train did not have to pick up any passengers (Republican votes), but it did have to make a few stops along the way (to meet with members of the GOP). Joe Biden, the conductor of that train, needed to be seen by the Democrats and everyone else as extending an olive branch across the aisle.

For everything to go his way, each faction had to perform in a way Biden predicted. For example, Joe Biden counted on the fact that his "friend" Mitch McConnell would strongly discourage any GOP support for the bill in the Senate. Biden knew the GOP's offer would be nowhere near his proposed plan and would be easy to reject (Republicans' top offer was a quarter of the size of Biden's proposed bill). The GOP offer was, of course, rejected immediately by the president.

Biden was sincere in inviting Republican lawmakers to the White House. He preferred to have all legislation pass on a bipartisan basis; however, Biden the pragmatist was not holding his breath. Even though he did not expect Republican support, he negotiated in good faith. As a decades-long veteran of the Senate and a two-term vice president, Biden knew the McConnell intransigence would likely guide the entire Republican caucus.

Biden knew how the game was played. Unlike other less experienced politicians, he saw the entire playing field. And he was willing to play along to get what he felt was so sorely needed in the United States: an enormous Covid-19 relief bill that would cut child poverty, help families in pain, and mitigate against Covid-19, among dozens of other important things. This was the largest spending bill of all time, just edging out the Tax Cut Act of 2017. Biden's new bill favored the bottom half of society, while the earlier GOP bill predominantly favored the rich and large corporations.

It may be difficult to envision Biden as this grand chesslike master. His folksy demeanor, which is authentic, causes many to underestimate him. From his first months in the Oval Office, he proved himself to be a strategic thinker who consistently executed on the strategies he employed.

Exhibit Patience and Discipline

Biden knew that he needed to keep the minimum wage legislation in the Covid-19 relief bill to satisfy the nearly 100 Progressives in his party. Biden the pragmatist, however, knew that if that provision was left in until the end, he would lose two Democratic votes. With a 50-50 split and Vice President Harris breaking any ties, Biden had no room for error. He needed all 50 Democrats for this bill to gain passage.

Nonetheless, he did not ask that the minimum wage provision be removed. He kept it in the bill right through the House vote at the end of February 2021. Biden was biding his time. It was as if with age he not only gained wisdom; he also became a more patient leader. And that patience was about to be rewarded: one day before the vital vote, the Senate parliamentarian made a key ruling that entailed stripping the minimum wage provision out of the Senate version of the final bill because it violated certain, specific rules of procedure (rules erected as guardrails to avoid blowing up the deficit).

The parliamentarian verdict against the minimum wage angered the Progressives in the caucus mightily. Several Progressive Democrats came out to rail against the Senate parliamentarian, a nonpartisan named Elizabeth MacDonough, who has served in that post since 2012 (she worked under both Democratic and Republican administrations).

The chair of the Progressive caucus, Pramila Jayapal, tweeted this strong statement out the night of the parliamentarian's ruling: "The Senate parliamentarian issues an advisory opinion. . . . The VP can overrule them—as has been done before. We should do EVERYTHING we can to keep our promise, deliver a $15 minimum wage, and give 27 million workers a raise."[1]

One of the other early, visible lawmakers against Mac-Donough was Representative Ilhan Omar of the 5th District of Minnesota, who called for the parliamentarian to be fired and replaced.

---

[1]Pramila Jayapal, Twitter, February 25, 2021.

Within a few days, twenty-three congressional Democrats wrote to Biden and Harris urging them to overturn the parliamentarian's decision. That was a nonstarter for President Biden, who came out days earlier to say he would abide by the Senate rules, no matter what. When it came to upholding and fighting for American norms and institutions, Biden was hoping for opportunities to demonstrate his affinity for the persistent and positive powers and levers of the United States government. Biden knew how badly American institutions had been mangled in the previous five years.

Biden dodged a bullet when Elizabeth MacDonough proved him right by stating that the wage provision had to be removed. With each passing month of Biden's first year in office, he became ever more capable of dodging bullets. He was emerging as a new brand of old leader molded in the image of a Franklin Delano Roosevelt. Both men wanted to accomplish great, big things to expand the American safety net.

Alluding often to "winning the future," Biden was in no way ready to give up the fight for the $15 minimum wage. He was intensely focused on this bill, and he knew the timing and venue was wrong for a minimum wage battle.

The day before Memorial Day weekend in 2021, in a speech delivered in Cleveland, Ohio (a red state), Biden once more argued for the $15 wage. One could reasonably conclude that he regarded the wage as a building block of any functioning, thriving American economy. He believed the minimum wage should not be a poverty wage, and he was determined to upgrade the status quo. But he was biding his time and leading with his top priorities—the ones he felt were most important and had the best chance of success.

Act "Decisively, Quickly, and Boldly"

On the day of the first House vote, the *New York Times* ran a piece about 2020 voters who voted for Trump but also supported the $1.9 trillion bill. The reporter interviewed far-right Republicans and asked Trump voters what they thought of the plan: "Most of it sounds like a good idea. . . . There's a lot of people that could use those checks," said Anthony McGill, a 52-year-old self-described conservative Republican from rural Maine.[2]

In the early hours of a February Saturday morning, the House voted on the $1.9 trillion plan and passed it. The final vote was 219-212, on a strict party line vote. Not a single House Republican voted for it, as Biden predicted.

Garnering the passage of this huge package was the first real test of his power, and Biden knew that nothing mattered until the Senate passed the bill. Given that his party controlled both chambers of Congress, if he failed to accomplish that, he knew his presidency might never recover from the blow.

The same week as the House voted on the bill, Biden took time to first celebrate the 50 million Covid-19 vaccines administered since taking office. However, Biden went to lengths to let Americans know that this was no time to take the virus lightly: "I want to make something clear. This is not a time to relax. We must keep washing our hands, stay socially distant, and for God's sake, wear a mask," pleaded Biden. "Some of our progress in this fight is because so many people are stepping up and doing those things. The worst thing we can do now is let our guard down."[3]

---

[2]Lisa Lerer, "Give Biden a Chance," *New York Times*, February 25, 2021.
[3]Joe Biden, Speech, February 25, 2021.

President Biden was also not going to let his guard down on another front, gaining passage for his mammoth relief package. And for that, he set his sights on the upper chamber, where one or two "surprises" threatened the bill's ultimate passage.

In a brief statement from the White House, Biden underscored how the bill would relieve suffering for many Americans: "[W]e have no time to waste. If we act now, decisively, quickly and boldly, we can finally get ahead of this virus, we can finally get our economy moving again. And the people of this country have suffered far too much for far too long. We must relieve that suffering. And the American Rescue Plan does just that. It relieves the suffering."[4]

The formerly gaffe-prone Joe Biden was staying on-message and uttering few gaffes. His team achieved that by urging Biden to do two things: stick to teleprompter scripts and keep things brief. For example, the statement above was part of a very compact 45-second "speech."

In the weeks leading up to the votes in Congress, with every prepared speech delivered by teleprompter, Biden hammered home the virtues of the $1.9 trillion plan. His adherence to a disciplined, well-crafted message helped to keep the American people focused on the Covid-19 relief package. Biden's discipline was also a reflection of the quality of the people he put in charge around him. A clever up-and-comer like Jen Psaki is one good example.

One day after the House vote, Biden put Jen Psaki and others on the Sunday morning political shows to further advance the bill's message. When Psaki was pressed about the lack of bipartisanship in the House vote, her answer was on-message.

---

[4]Joe Biden, Statement, The White House, February 28, 2021.

First, she pointed out that there were more bipartisan law-makers invited into the Biden White House than there were during the previous four years combined. She added that Biden remained receptive to all ideas that would strengthen the bill.

Next, she said that the bill would "help people bridge through this period-of-time, get them direct checks, reopen schools, get more vaccines in the arms of Americans." She emphasized, "We have not seen a substantive, big proposal in response back from Republicans. This is the scope of the problem and the scope of the kind of package we need to pass to address that."[5]

At the same time that Biden aides were making the rounds on the Sunday morning shows, Mitch McConnell was prom-ising zero Republican support for the bill in the Senate. His feet were set in cement. No argument mattered to him. He did not, however, represent the voice of the rest of the party.

Dozens of Republican state and local officials argued stren-uously *for* the bill. For example, Republican Oklahoma City Mayor David Holt called the package a "no-brainer," adding this: "[I]t's a very popular issue in my community regardless of your party registration. . . . [W]e think it's good public policy."[6]

McConnell pressed on with his opposition to the bill. Prior to the Senate vote, the minority leader called the bill "wildly expensive" and "largely unrelated to the problem."[7] Since sen-ators are not fact-checked like presidents, it is worth exam-ining the words of the Senate minority leader.

First, it is, at best, disingenuous of him to label the bill as "unrelated to the problem." The package included over $400 billion for lower-income families earning under $75,000; a boost in unemployment aid; and $350 billion for state, local,

[5]Jen Psaki, Interview with Dana Bash, *State of the Union*, CNN, February 28, 2021.
[6]David Holt, Interview, *CNN Newsroom with Poppy Harlow and Jim Sciutto*, CNN, February 27, 2021.
[7]Mitch McConnell, Press Briefing, March 2, 2021.

and tribal governments. It also included $60 billion for vaccinations and contact tracing and testing.

Another key to the bill was the $130 billion to safely reopen K–12 schools. By the spring of 2021 that was turning into an imperative. Research showed that a third of all students felt that their education was suffering badly throughout the pandemic. It also revealed once again how the poorest communities got hit the hardest. A McKinsey study found that students of color may have sacrificed six to twelve months of meaningful study.[8]

In sum, one could make the argument that the bill was too large, but one could not credibly say that the stimulus plan was "largely unrelated to the problem."

McConnell's intransigence helped to explain his low favorability rating, which stood at a paltry 19 percent. In stark contrast, Biden's favorability rating was 62 percent (and that was before the votes on the package). Of course, these favorability numbers rise and fall over time.

The Biden White House knew what those numbers represented: a real opportunity to pass meaningful legislation. And the Covid-19 relief package was the right legislation at the right time. In an average of polls, 71 percent of all Americans approved of the bill, making it the third most popular Washington bill of the past thirty years (behind only the Brady bill of 1993 and the vote to raise the minimum wage in 2007, which took effect in 2009).

Privately, Republicans were finally coming to terms with the realities of their strategy of simply bucking everything to come from the Biden administration. Rachel Bade, co-author of *The Politico Playbook*, explained that the Republicans running against Biden's policies was akin to the Democrats

---

[8]Emma Dorn et. al., "Covid-19 and Unfinished Business," McKinsey & Company, July 27, 2021.

running against the George W. Bush White House after 9/11. In the weeks and months after the attack in 2001, America was on a war footing. The Democrats had great difficulty fighting the GOP then.

Political reporters and the Biden administration in 2021 explained that battling Covid-19 was just like fighting a war—and that fueled real concern among GOP leadership, who recognized that the party was still smack in the middle of an identity crisis.

Make Good on Promises

During the 2020 presidential campaign, candidate Biden promised a far more robust response to Covid-19 and its ill effects on America. In fact, Covid-19 was one of the defining issues in the campaign. Most voters thought Biden would do a good job battling the pandemic.

Voters felt that Biden would make good on his promises, of which there were many. In addition to his stimulus package, Biden started work—as promised—on day one of his administration to correct some backward-looking policies implemented by the preceding administration. Put another way, he set out to right the Trump-wrongs he perceived as most destructive, the most contrary to American values and a true democracy.

On January 20, 2021, President Biden signed approximately a dozen executive orders and directives to reverse what he perceived as the most malignant mistakes of his predecessor. He signed 50 executive orders and actions in his first 50 days, outpacing all presidents who came before him. Of the 50, almost half were to overturn an order or directive made in the previous four years.

In signing these executive orders, Biden made good on many of the promises he made during the 2020 campaign. The most noteworthy of these actions included rejoining the Paris Climate Accords, stopping the U.S. exit from the World Health Organization (WHO), and shutting down the Keystone XL pipeline.

Other orders signed by Biden received less attention than those. Three such executive orders were classified as "equity" orders. Biden wanted equity across the board, as it pertained to voting, education, and gender equality. On accomplishing the latter, he established a White House Gender Equality Policy Council.

On key matters involving immigration and racial justice, President Biden revoked Trump policies that limited funding to cities that permitted Black Lives Matter protests and revoked a policy that prohibited legal immigration during Covid-19. He also extended the national suspension on evictions and foreclosures, and he lengthened the pause on student debt loan and interest through most of 2021.

The executive orders and proclamations that may have had the most impact were the actions he took on behalf of defeating Covid-19 and, more precisely, its negative economic consequences on tens of millions of families. In addition to keeping America in the World Health Organization and assigning Dr. Anthony Fauci as the head of the delegation to the WHO, he also created a new post that would report directly to Biden: Covid-19 response coordinator.

Several of Biden's promises took the form of lifting up those he felt were left behind in recent decades. Those Americans were those in poverty and others who worked several poor-paying jobs to keep food on the table. Covid-19 hastened the horrendous outcomes for the impoverished and people of color. Using tools like child tax credits, Joe Biden set out to give the poor a real shot at rising out of poverty. He wanted to help the lower and middle classes and his policies undergirded that most important promise.

Anticipate Surprises

Of course, a president can accomplish only so much with executive orders. Big, important pieces of legislation like the stimulus plan must be done through legislation and Congress.

On the day the historic stimulus bill was taken up by the Senate, the unthinkable happened—something that could have killed the bill and, along with it, Biden's chances of legislating effectively moving forward. Soon after the Senate started to take up the bill, a fissure in the Democratic caucus emerged, and the bill went from near-sure-thing to the verge of collapse. One senator—and it only takes one with a 50-50 Senate—objected to the language and stipulation found in one amendment related to the size and duration of unemployment benefits.

There is no need to get too much in the weeds. Suffice it to say the bill, and along with it, Biden's political capital, hung in the balance. The senior senator from West Virginia, Joe Manchin, the new kingmaker (or potential agenda-killer, depending upon one's perspective), had flexed his new power muscles for months. Manchin was the 50th vote, and without it, the bill would go down in flames and, along with it, the hopes and dreams of millions of Americans and business owners who really needed the money.

Here's how two reporters described his puzzling moves in *Politico*: "Manchin's outsized influence has cast its shadow over the Senate since the Democrats captured their scant 50-50 majority. He's already derailed a cabinet nominee and led the opposition to a federal $15 minimum wage even as his party's leaders pushed for it. But Friday was Manchin's most quintessential moment. The centrist Democrat paralyzed the entire Senate for more than ten hours and threatened to side with Republicans seeking to cut weeks of unemployment benefits."[9]

As a result of the 11th-hour Manchin power play and ensuing half-day delay, turmoil seemed to descend on a nation already on pins and needles. Ten hours might not seem like much, but this happened on a Friday when all senators were stuck in Washington, D.C., for the weekend (rather than be with their families back home in their districts). As a result, the Manchin blowback took on an outsized proportion. The relief bill was incredibly popular, and Manchin's move caused a great deal of anxiety throughout the nation.

Manchin's behavior also confused some senators closest to him. For example, Krysten Sinema, his co-moderate who also voted against the minimum wage hike, practically begged Manchin to vote for the package. So did Jon Tester, the Democratic senator from Montana. It may have been the junior senator from his state of West Virginia, Republican Shelley Moore Capito, who summed it up best when questioned by a reporter: "I have no idea what he's doing, to be quite frank. Maybe you can tell me."[10]

One other prominent Republican that really hammered what Manchin did was the governor of his own state, Republican Jim Justice. "I still believe that we need go big or not go at all, because we have too many people across especially West Virginia that are hurting. What was written in the law

---

[9]Burgess Everett and Marianne Levine, "No Idea What He's Doing: Manchin Perplexes with Covid-19 Aid Play," *Politico*, March 5, 2021.
[10]Ibid.

was written by Joe Manchin. He doesn't care about you," he remarked viciously.[11]

It is worth repeating here: this was the Republican governor of a ruby-red state, Manchin's state, that Trump won by forty points, excoriating a Democrat who delayed a bill that every Republican senator voted to reject.

That was a relatively rare event, but it pointed out the schism between Washington, D.C., and the rest of the country. The disconnect between state officials and federal lawmakers has seldom been greater. In D.C. even a Covid-19 relief bill is seen as a political bargaining chip to make the Democratic president and Democratic Senate look bad. But local officials on the ground throughout the country knew how much this aid was needed, and many spoke out.

During the ten-hour delay in the Senate, Joe Biden made several public statements from the White House about the relief package. He stressed that the United States was still 9.5 million jobs down from a year earlier. He said it would take two years just to get back to where the country was in 2020. "We can't afford one step forward and two steps backward," reasoned Biden. "People need the help now."

Biden was not only talking to the American people. He was also, behind the scenes, working the phones, talking to Joe Manchin. And those conversations occurred more than once. All the talks paid off. Joe Manchin was finally on board.

Reaching a deal with Manchin cleared the way for a 50-49 vote, strictly along party lines. But it was done. *Biden was able to get the largest piece of legislation in history passed in the Senate, and he accomplished it with a 50-50 split.*

Biden started out asking for $1.9 trillion, and he ended up getting $1.9 trillion. That rarely happens in the U.S.

---

[11]Jim Justice, Interview, CNN, March 9, 2021.

government, a vast bureaucracy characterized by visceral divisiveness.

Senate Democrats were thrilled, applauding the final vote in a rare moment of celebration in which Biden chalked up a huge victory, while Mitch McConnell and his caucus went down in defeat. The former Senate majority leader had not suffered any big losses since he took over the speakership in the first days of January 2015. Six years is a long time before tasting blood in one's mouth. McConnell might have forgotten the taste.

Either way, this is how the combative, less powerful Senate minority leader viewed what some were calling a lifeline to the poorest in society: "It was a multi-trillion trojan horse full of bad old liberal ideas."[12] It killed former Majority Leader Mitch McConnell to see his power sucked away and used on something that he viewed as frivolous as helping poorer Americans and people of color. In his version of America, those goals were not only unnecessary; they hurt the country.

Celebrate Wins

After the bill passed the Senate, Biden issued a statement through Press Secretary Jen Psaki that included the following: "This agreement allows us to move forward on the urgently needed American Rescue Plan with $1,400 relief checks, funding we need to finish this vaccine rollout, open schools and end the suffering from the pandemic and more."[13]

After the successful vote, no one seemed happier than Senate Majority Leader Chuck Schumer, who, along with

---

[12]Mitch McConnell, Interview, *The Story*, Fox News, March 3, 2021.
[13]Jen Psaki, Press Statement on Behalf of President, The White House, March 5, 2021.

President Biden, helped to broker the Manchin negotiation and celebrated a long-awaited and rare legislative win. Schumer said this elatedly about the $1.9 trillion plan: "[W]e have fulfilled that promise. Now nobody said passing one of the largest, perhaps the most significant bills to help the poor and working people in decades was going to be easy . . . but it is done." He continued: "We were not going to let anything stop us until we got the job done and by God, we did . . . . [T]he secret to the success here, is the caucus unifying. Every person realizing that we needed every other person to have this victory. . . . [W]e don't let our differences stop us from achieving success."[14] In responding to questions, Schumer reminded the press that Democrats did not hibernate or shut everything down under Trump. He said that Democrats worked hard to get things done under the previous administration.

The senior senator from Ohio, Democrat Sherrod Brown, called the legislation bipartisan among the people of the nation, even though the Senate vote garnered zero bipartisan votes in Congress. He called it "the best thing we have done in the Senate in my career. . . . [V]oters in the summer of 2021 are going to say I voted for Joe Biden and my life got better," concluded Brown.[15]

The morning of the successful Senate vote, a jubilant Joe Biden said this in front of cameras at the White House: "This nation has suffered too much, for much too long. And everything in this package is designed to relieve the suffering and to meet the most urgent needs of the nation and put us in a better position to prevail." Biden proclaimed proudly, "I promised the American people that help is on the way. Today I can say we have taken one more giant step forward in delivering on that

---

[14]Chuck Schumer, Speech, March 6, 2021.
[15]Sherrod Brown, Interview with Frederica Whitfield, CNN, March 6, 2021.

promise. . . . [T]his plan will get checks out the door starting this month to the American people who so desperately need the help; many of whom are lying in their bed at night staring at the ceiling wondering will I lose my job if I haven't already? Will I lose my insurance? Will I lose my home? Over eighty-five percent of American households will get direct payments of $1,400 per person."[16]

When, after the tumult surrounding the Senate passage of the vote, Biden was asked what the prior 24 hours and the Manchin drama say about the next four years, he answered: "They are going to be good. . . . [W]e are going to succeed moving forward. Look, the American people strongly support what we are doing. That's the key here. And that's going to continue to seep down through the public, including from our Republican friends. [There] are a lot of Republicans who came very close, who got a lot of pressure on them, and I still haven't given up on getting their support," answered Biden hopefully.[17]

Start a Revolution

After the Senate bill passed, it had to go back to the House, since the bill had been altered in the upper chamber of Congress. But Democrats weren't worried a bit. They knew that the bill was on a fast track to President Biden's desk. After the near debacle with Manchin, Chuck Schumer would not have gotten ahead of his skis without checking with Nancy Pelosi. He had to be sure that what he promised, and gained in the Senate, would be enough for the House to pass the bill. Perhaps

---

[16]Joe Biden, Remarks, The White House, March 6, 2021.
[17]Ibid.

one of the three most skilled politicians in the country, no one held a caucus together more sure-handedly than the San Francisco speaker of the house, Nancy Pelosi.

Even before the House could vote, Treasury Secretary Janet Yellen said publicly and visibly, "[T]his is a tremendously important package that will bring hundreds of millions of Americans the relief they need. First . . . it will provide the money we need to vaccinate our population to get the pandemic under control. It will provide the resources that schools need to operate safely."[18] Then Yellen, the first woman Treasury secretary, extolled the virtues of the checks that she felt would help propel the economy forward.

On day 50 of Biden's administration, the House took a second and final vote on the historic stimulus, anti-Covid-19, anti-poverty bill (those characterizations were how Team Biden sold the package). The House passed the $1.9 trillion bill along Democratic and party lines, 220-211. After the bill was passed by both chambers of Congress, several in the press referred to the bill as "transformative," "transformational," and "a policy revolution."

This is what President Biden said as he signed the bill into law: "This historic legislation is about rebuilding back the backbone of this country and giving people in this nation, working people, middle class folks, people who built this country a fighting chance."[19]

Biden understood that there needed to be as little time as possible between the signing of the bill and its implementation, and in a package that size, there was a great deal to implement.

---

[18]Janet Yellen, Interview, MSNBC, March 8, 2021.
[19]Joe Biden, Remarks, The White House, March 11, 2021.

The first step that Americans would feel with real impact were those $1,400 checks. In stark contrast to his predecessor, President Biden insisted that his name *not* go on the checks. That simple change spoke volumes about the differences between the two men. Joe Biden did not want there to be any delay in getting the American people the funds he knew were so desperately needed.

Biden also knew there was not a moment to lose because of several other pressing reasons. Perhaps most important, on the day the bill was signed into law, 75 percent of Americans backed the record-breaking bill, according to a *Politico/ Morning Consult* poll. The president had three of every four Americans squarely behind him—and equally important—they were behind his decision to go as big as he did. Joe Biden knew that there was no guarantee that his favorable approval math would last forever. Biden remembered how the 2009 relief package of Obama's presidency diminished in popularity as Republicans constantly took their shots at the bill. Biden was determined not to suffer the same consequence.

Obsess Over Implementation

Joe Biden knew he needed an exceptional individual to implement all the stipulations—the promises—he made in that $1.9 trillion package. What good are promises unless someone has the responsibility of making sure that all provisions of the bill are fulfilled?

Biden was in a unique position to choose the right person who would help him make the provisions of the plan come to life. That is because he was the one President Obama selected for such a role when Biden was a newly minted vice president in 2009.

Sometimes looking back can help a leader move forward. Examining Joe Biden's approach to dealing with the relief bill of 2009 tells us how he would sell the bill in 2021.

Within a month of the Obama plan passing Congress, Obama offered more detail on just what he expected Biden to accomplish: "As part of his duty, Joe will keep an eye on how precious tax dollars are being spent," Obama said. "To you, he's Mr. Vice President. But around the White House we call him 'the sheriff,' because if you're misusing taxpayer dollars, you'll have to answer to him."[20]

Back in 2009, aides to Biden described him as "obsessed with implementation." Biden held weekly meetings with local leaders, mayors, and governors. According to Ron Klain, his chief of staff at the time (and again when Biden became president), "The vice president insisted that the recovery implementation office that reported to him . . . had what he called the 24-hour rule, which is any question that a governor or a mayor raised got an answer within 24 hours."[21]

Fast-forward to 2021, and here is how President Biden emphasized the need for sound execution of the plan, speaking from the Rose Garden of the White House: "It's one thing to pass the American Rescue Plan, it's going to be another to implement it. It's going to require fastidious oversight to make sure there is no waste or fraud. And the law does what it's designed to do. I mean it. We have to get this right. *Details matter.*"[22]

President Biden knew he needed to appoint someone with his level of urgency and obsession to detail. He needed an experienced, proven leader. He found that in the person

---

[20]Barack Obama, Interview with Asma Khalid, NPR, WBEZ, Chicago, April 12, 2020.
[21]Asma Khalid, NPR, WBEZ, Chicago, April 12, 2020.
[22]Joe Biden, Remarks, The White House, March 12, 2021; emphasis added.

of Gene Sperling, who had served on the economic teams of Presidents Clinton and Obama as head of the National Economic Council.

Sperling, who earlier in his career had argued for more fiscal conservatism, felt strongly that the kind of overwhelming stimulus package that Biden passed was necessary to get the economy back on track. He was one of many officials who pushed back on the Larry Summers' op-ed that stated that the bill was too large in scope and dollars.

According to a White House spokesperson, "Sperling will work with leaders of White House policy councils and other key agencies to get funds out quickly, speed up the administration's work to battle the coronavirus pandemic and will partner with state and local governments."[23]

How high on Biden's list was Gene Sperling? High enough for a cabinet level position. It turns out that Sperling was being considered for the Office of Management and Budget (OMB) after Neera Tanden failed to win Senate confirmation in February 2021.

To implement and oversee the various aspects of his package, President Biden obviously did not choose his vice president as Obama did during the Great Recession. This did not cause a stir in the press. In fact, it was difficult to find any media mentions of the difference in policy implementation between Obama and Biden.

There were two key reasons Biden likely decided against enlisting his vice president as the Covid-19 relief implementation czar. First, he needed her to help govern the country. He thought she and the second gentleman would do a great job of helping to sell the stimulus plan across the nation.

---

[23]Laura Barron Lopez and Ben White, "Biden Taps Gene Sperling," *Politico*, March 14, 2021.

Second, and more important, he did not want to bog her down with a second full-time job. Joe Biden knew, from his own experience, that overseeing the implementation of the bill was a huge, demanding task. He had even bigger things in mind for his capable vice president.

Biden once said "that the hardest thing to do as a leader is the thing that prevents the worst consequence because the public won't really give you credit for it; they won't pay attention to it. And that's what [a leader is] trying to do, prevent the worst consequence in all of these issues, all of it of course happening at the same time."[24]

To make sure Americans knew of the best parts of the bill for the American electorate, Biden planned a "Help Is Here" tour. Biden decided on Pennsylvania as his first stop.

Persuade Constituents and Finish Strong

The effort to sell the bill to the American people got underway almost immediately. And it was an ambitious effort. Within days of final passage of the bill, after Pennsylvania, Biden and his team planned stops for himself in Atlanta and Delaware County and for Jill Biden in Vermont. Biden's plan was to take his bill to the towns across the heartland and across the country. He wanted to be sure that the American people understood the majority of the merits of his record-making legislation.

Events were quickly planned for Kamala Harris and Doug Emhoff in Denver and Las Vegas and for the second

[24]Evan Osnos, Interview on Joe Biden, *New Day*, CNN, March 26, 2021.

gentleman alone in New Mexico. Other surrogates hit the air-waves. Biden wanted, and got, an all-hands-on-deck response to sell the bill from coast to coast.

There were so many aspects to the Biden $1.9 trillion package. Benefits like child tax credits and other stipulations needed to be explained and discussed with the people receiving the money. This was the type of politicking that Biden excelled at—retail politics with a full helping of empathy. It involved Joe Biden speaking with a few people at a time, which Biden loved to do. For the most part, it did not involve big, important, sweeping speeches.

"There are a lot of people who use the term 'victory lap' in a derogatory way," exclaimed House Majority Whip Jim Clyburn (D-S.C.), a Biden friend and confidante. "I've already heard people saying that Biden is about to take a victory lap. Well, that's a lot of crap. One of the—if not the biggest—mistake[s] that Obama made, in my opinion, was getting the Recovery Act done and not explaining to people what he had done."[25]

As a result of all of Biden's actions, people were feeling more optimistic about the future than at any time since the Covid-19 crisis hit the United States a year earlier. When the pandemic started to bite down on America in April 2020, only 17 percent of Americans thought the worst was behind them. By mid-March 2021, that number had more than quadrupled to 77 percent.[26]

Drilled down, the numbers certainly reflected more enthusiasm for the bill among Republicans in the country than Republicans in Congress. Almost 60 percent of self-identified Republicans wanted the Covid-19 bill, and only

[25]Christopher Cadelago and Natasha Korecki, "The Biden Blitz Is Coming," *Politico*, March 9, 2021.
[26]SSRS Poll, CNN, March 2021.

35 percent opposed it, according to the same *Politico/Morning Consult* poll taken a day or two before the final House vote.

On the night President Biden signed the bill into law, he implored the American people, with humility and empathy, to help him extinguish the virus: "I will not relent until we beat the virus . . . but I need you, the American people. I need you. I need every American to do their part. And that's not hyperbole. I need you. I need you to get vaccinated when it's your turn and when you can find an opportunity. And to help your family, your friends, your neighbors get vaccinated as well. Because here's the point. If we do all this, if we do our part, if we do this together, by July the fourth, there's a good chance you, your families and friends, will be able to get together in your backyard or in your neighborhood and have a cookout or a barbecue and celebrate Independence Day. That doesn't mean large events with lots of people together, but it does mean small groups will be able to get together. After this long hard year, that will make this Independence Day something truly special, where we not only mark our independence as a nation, but we begin to mark our independence from this virus. I will not relent until we beat this virus, but I need you, the American people."[27]

President Biden was successful in mobilizing the American people, from healthcare workers to his fellow citizens. He helped to get shots in arms at an unprecedented rate. In his first 100 days, more than half of the adult population (130 million people) had received at least one shot. He accomplished this by averaging more than 3 million shots a day, despite the pause in administering the Johnson & Johnson vaccine (due to blood clots in a handful of women). That FDA pause lasted less than two weeks.

---

[27]Joe Biden, Address to the Nation, The White House, March 11, 2021.

There was one other huge reason that made this huge bill such a significant potential win for President Biden and, more important, the American people. This bill was being lauded as one of the greatest government achievements to help the poorest and middle class in decades, including hundreds of Black and Brown communities, as well as towns and cities that catered to the 85 percent of all Americans who earned less than $80,000 per year.

Here is how the *Washington Post* put it: "The roughly $1.9 trillion American Rescue Plan, which only Democrats supported, spends most of the money on low-income and middle-class Americans and state and local governments, with very-little funding going toward companies. The plan is one of the largest federal responses to a downturn Congress has enacted."[28] The same newspaper pointed out that the huge aid bill would help Black farmers in a way no legislation had since the Civil Rights Act of 1964, more than half a century earlier.

At about the same time, members of the GOP were calling the $1.9 trillion bill a "liberal wish list," "left of Lenin," and chock full of "Socialist policies." House minority leader Kevin McCarthy said this of the bill in the well of Congress: "It showers money on special interest. It's a laundry list of left-wing priorities that predate the pandemic."[29]

Wyoming senator and leading Republican voice John Barrasso described the bill like this: "[T]o call this Covid-19 relief is really false advertising. Only nine percent of the money actually goes to defeating the virus. . . . [T]his is a Nancy Pelosi payoff to the liberal, liberal left." When the moderator of the program pointed out that a billion dollars was going to help

[28]Heather Long, Alyssa Flowers, and Andrew Van Dam, "Biden Stimulus Showers Money on Americans," *Washington Post*, March 6, 2021.
[29]Kevin McCarthy, House Speech, U.S. House of Representatives, March 10, 2021.

Wyoming, Barrasso pointed to big money going to "Blue states and failed pension programs." He also accused Democrats of allocating funds to states corruptly. In addition, he sprinkled in a few other key Republican talking points. Barrasso said the bill was not supposed to be about $1,400 to illegal immigrants or $1,400 checks to felons who are behind bars . . . or block grants to Sanctuary cities or monies to schools that continue to stay closed." He proclaimed that these things represented "just the tip of the iceberg of what's wrong with this bill."[30]

A few days before Barrasso uttered those words, Democratic Representative Tim Ryan of Ohio had heard enough from those "obstructionist Republicans." He was irate and bellowed this out in the well of the House: "Heaven forbid we pass something that's going to help the damned-workers in the United States of America. Stop talking about Dr. Seuss and start working with us on behalf of the American workers."[31] (Some Republicans were televised reading Dr. Seuss during the relief bill debate, preferring to discussing anything other than the bill.)

When Biden's predecessor spent $2.3 trillion on a tax cut in 2017—in the Tax Cut and Jobs Act (TCJA)—the bulk of the money went to the nation's top 20 percent, and more than half of the money went to the richest 5 percent. There was some outcry from Democrats back then, particularly the Bernie Sanders' Progressive wing of the Democratic party. Ruby-red-Republicans like Senator Barrasso loved that legislation.

The two plans were intended to reach two separate segments of American society. However, Biden's American Rescue Plan had two important things in common with Trump's TCJA. First, the price tag of Biden's plan was in the

[30]John Barrasso, Interview, *This Week with George Stephanopoulos*, March 14, 2021.
[31]Tim Ryan, House Speech, U.S. House of Representatives, March 9, 2021.

same general $2 trillion neighborhood as Trump's tax cut. Second, and more indicative of the divisiveness in Congress, neither plan received any votes from the opposing party. Not one Democratic lawmaker voted for the Trump tax cut, and similarly, no Republican lawmaker voted for Biden's Covid-19 relief bill (that was also true with Obamacare, which received zero GOP support and is now regarded as popular).

Differing ideologies played a role in helping to understand the two biggest differences of the plans. The Trump plan overhauled the tax plan in the most drastic way in over 30 years. It had the greatest effect on earners making more than $200,000 per year. It was also a huge giveaway for corporations, by lowering their tax burden from 35 percent to 21 percent. Put another way, Republicans and Democrats had spectacularly divergent views on how federal money should be spent.

Of the two plans, one was aimed at corporations and the most affluent, and the other plan was aimed at those on the lowest rungs of society, those most adversely affected by the pandemic. Unlike the $1.9 trillion plan, most of the previous legislation that enlarged the government's outreach and widened the safety net was bipartisan (e.g., the 1935 Social Security Act).

President Biden didn't care how he did it; he only cared that he got it done. The day after he signed the bill into law, Joe Biden said in a Rose Garden celebration that this was the greatest bill to help children since World War II.

There was one other reason that Biden did not sweat the fact that his bill was not bipartisan in Congress: the soaring popularity of the relief package throughout the country. Even about half of Republican constituents supported it, and about seven out of ten Americans favored the plan.

"Since taking office," exclaimed the *Washington Post*, "Biden has outlined a sweeping agenda that has delighted members of the party's liberal wing, who were skeptical that a former Senate institutionalist known for moderation would push through policies aimed at transforming the nation. The first big victory came this past week, when Democrats approved an expansive $1.9 trillion coronavirus relief bill containing numerous long-sought liberal initiatives. 'It is absolutely a bold and transformative and progressive agenda,' said Rep. Pramila Jayapal (D-Wash.), chair of the Congressional Progressive Caucus. 'Where candidate Joe Biden started is different from where President Joe Biden started.'"[32]

The comment by Jayapal is worthy of elaboration. Biden campaigned from a center-left position. The first two bills he put forward, however, were the most progressive since Franklin Roosevelt (as he had promised Bernie Sanders during the campaign).

After fifty days of the new Biden administration, Democrats had a swell of confidence and a wave of unbridled enthusiasm they had not felt in years. Since 2015 Mitch McConnell had ruled the Republican roost, and along with it, controlled the congressional agenda. He delighted in dealing Democrats defeat after defeat. That is one of the reasons Biden's victory was so sweet for Democrats.

But more important to Biden was the groundswell of support for the package across the United States. Unlike his predecessor's tax cut plan of 2017, Biden's plan did great things for the bottom 40 percent of the country and cut poverty significantly, especially in communities of color.

Biden felt that—due to the popularity of the $1.9 trillion plan—Republican voters would finally inflict pain on members of the GOP. Almost all Democratic voters and half of Republicans favored the grand bill. It was popular in most districts

---

[32]Ashley Parker and Matt Viser, "Biden's Sweeping Ambitions Delight Liberals," *Washington Post,* March 13, 2021.

in America. Joe Biden had a 62 percent approval rating, while McConnell had an approval rating of 19 percent (House leader Kevin McCarthy had a 21 percent approval rating).

All that evidence led one senior Biden advisor to conclude that lawmakers could not just oppose everything with impunity, especially during a pandemic. According to the Democratic strategist Mike Donilon, Republicans did not fully grasp just how bad their no-vote-to-free-money-and-other-goodies was going to hurt the Republican brand and their chances to pick up seats in the 2022 mid-terms.

What evidence did Donilon have for predicting a spillage of Republican party blood? In a memo, circulated at the White House, Donilon stated that there was ample evidence that this resistance would be "quite damaging" to the Republican party. He pointed to the fact that approval of Republicans dropped five points since the election, and that overall GOP favorability hovered at around 30 percent (less than half of Biden's approval numbers). "Opposing President Biden's American Rescue Plan only exacerbates Republicans' predicament," reasoned Donilon. "The GOP is putting itself at odds with a rescue package supported overwhelmingly by the American people."[33]

The memo concluded with this summary: "[T]he country is looking for action. For progress. For solutions. On COVID-19. On the economy. You see it and hear it all over the country. Voters are hurting—and they're looking for leadership that comes forward with plans and solutions. This is not a moment in the country when obstructionism will be rewarded."[34]

For Mitch McConnell, the jig was up. He was revealed for what he was: a hyper-partisan who had promised not to work with the Democrats or Joe Biden. When it came to big pieces

---

[33]Mike Donilon, Memo, The White House, February 16, 2021.
[34]Ibid.

of legislation; McConnell wanted to be deeply involved with substantial legislation, but only Republican legislation.

Joe Biden knew what steps he needed to take next to ensure that the plan he persuaded constituents to accept did what it was intended to accomplish. He never wavered from his goal of helping the people who most needed him.

Be Memorable

During the 2020 presidential race, after Joe Biden secured the Democratic nomination, there was a telephone call that took place between him and Bernie Sanders, according to Biden biographer Evan Osnos. According to Osnos's source, a senior aide to Bernie Sanders, Joe Biden told the Vermont senator that he wanted "to be the most progressive president since FDR [Franklin Delano Roosevelt]."[35]

A year after that phone conversation, Biden was an occupant of the White House, Sanders was the chair of the Senate Budget Committee, and presidential historians find themselves in great demand on cable airwaves and network interviews. Getting the near $2 trillion bill certainly helped Biden's legacy. He could not have been more sure-footed out of the gate. He was wearing his experience well.

Michael Beschloss, an American historian with a Harvard MBA who has authored nine books on the presidency, was effusive in his praise of Biden after the Covid-19 bill passed: "He's delivering. Look at the problems he has had to deal with. The pandemic above all, and the economic suffering that is widespread, along with threats to democracy. He's had to deal

---

[35]Evan Osnos, *Joe Biden: The Life, the Run, and What Matters Now*, Scribner, 2020, p. 13.

with all of that . . . and history usually honors a president who has to deal with fundamental crises."[36]

Beschloss then reasoned that the grandchildren of tomorrow will be reading about the passage of the transformative bill—Biden's bill—because the suffering that stretched from coast to coast had been as severe and as widespread as anything in generations (including the Great Recession of 2007–2009). He also pointed to the half-million people who were killed by the Covid-19 virus. He then complimented Joe Biden for using the full weight of the U.S. government to help fellow Americans protect themselves.

"Where have we seen that before?" Beschloss asked. "[The year] 1933 when Franklin Roosevelt came in. Joe Biden is a person of great modesty. He'd be the first to say he's not an FDR. But the reason we honor FDR is he came in with one third of America unemployed, huge suffering, people needing all sorts of help. And Roosevelt said I am going to go to use the federal government and go to Congress as quickly as possible. I am trying to relieve that suffering and make things better. This week reminds me of Roosevelt," explained Beschloss.[37]

Michael Beschloss was not the only presidential historian to see parallels between FDR and Biden. Pulitzer Prize–winning biographer and noted historian Jon Meacham knew well of the contributions of President Roosevelt. FDR came into office amid the Depression and four years after the Great Crash of 1929. It was a most precarious period in the United States and around the world (Adolph Hitler came to power the same year as FDR—1933).

Months before the 2020 presidential election in a *Washington Post* op-ed, Meacham wrote that, like Biden, FDR had come

---

[36]Michael Beschloss, CNN, March 10, 2021.
[37]Ibid.

to the presidency "in the bleakest of hours." He also wrote of the uncertainty that was swirling throughout the country: "No one knew whether the world as it was known could long endure amid destabilizing unemployment, Dust Bowl dislocations and plummeting confidence in the familiar American order." As Meacham explained, thanks to Roosevelt, America conquered the Nazis and Japanese imperialism, and the U.S. constitution and economy prevailed. Meacham made this argument for voting for Joe Biden during the 2020 campaign: "Now, in our own extraordinary moment, facing pandemic and panic, we are desperate for the steadying hand that Roosevelt offered America not so very long ago."[38]

Joe Biden may not turn out to be a Franklin Roosevelt. Few presidents occupy that very top tier in the ranked stratosphere of American leaders. However, the two men did have one key goal they hoped to achieve: to use the levers and mechanisms of the U.S. government to help Americans in pain.

For FDR, the Great Depression called for extreme measures and action—the New Deal. The programs and laws enacted under that umbrella consisted of a series of public works programs, financial overhauls, and other programs to help the unemployed, farmers, the handicapped, hungry children in families lacking a father. His administration also enacted the Social Security Administration (1935), an enormous program that serves as a lifeline to seniors to this day.

Thanks to Franklin Roosevelt's extraordinary accomplishments in the first 100 days of his presidency, all presidents are now judged by what they can accomplish in their first 100 days. Consequently, Joe Biden promised that he would get 100 million shots in American arms in the first 100 days of his

---

[38]Jon Meacham, Op-Ed, "Choosing a President Under a State of Siege," *Washington Post*, March 20, 2020.

presidency. In fact, he did it in 58 days, with 200 million shots in total before day 95.

How did Biden accomplish such a bold initiative? His administration had implemented a fact-based Covid-19 policy and acted in a way the previous administration did not. Biden assembled a top-tier team of scientists that delivered three informative briefings per week. He made sure that the Centers for Disease Control (CDC) was the preeminent disease institution it once was (politics had played an outsized role with the CDC under Trump). In addition, Biden always wore a mask (except when making remarks or speeches) and urged his fellow Americans to do the same. He also thanked all members of the CDC when he visited there in his third month of office.

Biden's efforts paid off almost immediately. In less than two months, the number of Covid-19 cases, and more important deaths, were down by 80 percent from just two months earlier. In the spring of 2021, scientists urged all Americans to get vaccinated as soon as it was their turn to do so, as there was a race between the vaccines and the variants. Biden provided the proverbial light at the end of the tunnel, even in the face of states like Texas that sought to undermine his efforts.

What's the Takeaway?

- **Think and Plan Strategically.** Leaders must demonstrate their capacity to see the big picture, the entire metaphorical chessboard, all at once. Biden had an overall strategy of uniting the nation and showing Americans that a broken government could work once again. When he knew that no Republicans would vote to pass his American Rescue bill, he shifted tactics by working behind the scenes to get all 50 Democratic senators on board.

- **Follow the 24-Hour Rule.** When Biden was vice president and in charge of implementation of President Obama's relief bill, he adhered to one key rule: answer every phone call or email from local government officials (e.g., governors and mayors) within 24 hours. That directive works well for every professional in government or business and is a key to enhancing the odds of successfully executing strategies.

- **Aim for the Highest, Always.** In Joe Biden's first year as president, he strived to get more than $6 trillion passed in three momentous bills. That was a huge challenge, particularly in an environment of hyper-partisanship. The degree of difficulty never caused Biden to back down.

CHAPTER 3

Value Specific Experience

We know nothing of what will happen in the future, but by the analogy of experience.

—Abraham Lincoln, Speech to the House of Representatives, 1839

Joe Biden was sworn in when he was 78 years old, the oldest president elected in history.[1] Never in the history of the United States had the *most* experienced president followed the *least* experienced president into office. Donald Trump had no political or military experience upon taking office. He was not a lawyer. He only worked in the family business of building and branding at a privately held company where he got to make all the rules. (In fact, many of his businesses had failed, from his casinos to Trump University, Steaks, Water, etc.) Barack Obama, who met with Trump when Trump was the president-elect, was stunned by Trump's general lack of knowledge of the world. He was "stupefied," according to an Obama senior advisor after the two had met.

In living-color contrast, by the time he entered office, Joe Biden had more years of political experience than any of the forty-five individuals who preceded him. He spent thirty-six years in the Senate and eight years as vice president to a moderate Democratic president. The contrast between the two men could not be more apparent.

---

[1] Biden was older than Ronald Reagan was after Reagan had served two terms in office.

Understand the Importance of Experience

Before examining how Joe Biden approached the highest office in the land, let us take a step back to see how previous presidents got there. Most of our 46 presidents had experience in more than just one profession. Many had substantial, packed résumés.

Prior to 2016, 70 percent of U.S. presidents had military experience, and 60 percent were lawyers. When it came to political experience, about 40 percent of presidents first served in the House of Representatives, 40 percent in the U.S. Senate, and 40 percent as state governors.

A third of presidents served as vice presidents—15 in total. All four of the top 10 presidents as ranked by most historians over the years—Thomas Jefferson, Theodore Roosevelt, Harry Truman, and Lyndon Johnson—were vice presidents, with the first two constituting half of the presidents on Mount Rushmore.

Could their experiences as vice president have served as a kind of apprenticeship to becoming president? Does that account for their success? Or did they have great teachers and mentors? Or did they have a combination of both?

Was President Biden's experience and political record, which some regard as "baggage," an asset or a liability to his readiness to lead upon coming into the Oval Office? Was the experience he had in political life directly transferable to the skills required of a president? What experiences prepared Biden to deal with a crisis like Covid-19? Was he well-suited to solve the crisis and ensuing financial dislocation? Exploring some of the research on leadership and the development of expertise will help us answer these questions.

In the 1980s, three researchers led by Morgan McCall of the Center for Creative Leadership in Greensboro, North Carolina, created a learning development model that is still respected to this day. It is known the world over as the 70-20-10 Leadership Development Model.[2]

This model was developed by studying successful managers and leaders. The researchers determined from their study that 70 percent of the knowledge of performing a job effectively comes from the experience gained *doing that precise job*. The researchers discovered that "challenging assignments" were the most useful predictors of future performance. In addition, 20 percent of the knowledge of performing a job comes from exchanges with other people, and 10 percent is learned from formal education or company training. The 70-20-10 model is still taught at many business schools around the globe, and hundreds of corporations around the world are guided by the model.

Adding to these findings, in 1993, K. Anders Ericsson of Florida State University presented data that became important to the developing field of what it takes to become an expert at most anything.[3] His study was conducted in conjunction with two colleagues at the exclusive Berlin Academy of Music. The research focused on student violinists and how they progressed throughout their childhood and young adulthood vis-à-vis their level of practice and level of expertise achieved. The research, quite bold at the time, argued this point: Thousands of hours—possibly *10,000 hours*—of "deliberate practice" (specific to an industry, specialty, or skill) are required to turn an adequate anybody into an extraordinary somebody. The three authors also cited *ten years* as the other related variable determinant of mastering a skill or vocation.

The original 1993 body of Anders Ericsson research was popularized in two different books, fifteen years after the

[2]Morgan McCall, et.al., *The Career Architect Development Planner*, 1996.
[3]The Morgan McCall Research first appeared in The American Psychological Association, McCall, et. al., The Role of Deliberate Practice in the Acquisition of Expert Performance, Vol. 100. No. 3, 363–406, 1993.

original research was published. Released in 2008, Malcolm Gladwell's *Outliers* and Geoffrey Colvin's *Talent Is Overrated* were both published to mostly rave reviews.[4] These two books were published at the same time. Both set out to find and explain just what it was that made the best of the best succeed at an extremely high level. What did the best do that differentiated themselves from the vast majority of those who performed adequately or even well?

Understand That "Talent Is Overrated"

Gladwell's *Outliers* and Colvin's *Talent Is Overrated* changed the way people think about expertise. According to them, we do not live in a world in which gifted people, with innate talent, simply emerge as the best in their fields. At the very least, successful people, and by extension leaders, must work incredibly hard to become great at anything.

Most leadership professionals agree with this logic. According to leadership professor Shayne Thomas, "[T]here's no such thing as a natural born leader. Sure, leadership may come easier to some people than others, but even those people need to fine tune their skills every now and then. In this way, you could say that leadership is not a 'one-and-done' acquired skill; it's something that people need to learn and constantly work on."[5]

Geoffrey Colvin had a high confidence level in the Anders Ericsson research and quoted it extensively: "What the authors

---

[4]Both books have been reprinted more than 150 times, combined in hardcover and paperback, likely putting both in the top 5 percent of all nonfiction books for more than a decade.

[5]Shayne Thomas, "There's No Such Thing as a Born Leader," *Cornerstone*, August 6, 2020.

call 'deliberate practice' makes all the difference. Or as they stated it with stark clarity in their scholarly paper, 'the differences between expert performers and normal adults reflects a life-long period of deliberative effort to improve performance in a given domain.'"[6] Colvin also pointed out that the same level of specific practice can play a role in making a team or organization as expert as an individual.[7] Malcolm Gladwell also concluded, "The people at the very top don't just work harder or even much harder than everyone else, they work much, *much* harder."[8]

Years after Gladwell's bestselling *Outliers* was published, Anders Ericsson along with new researchers contended that several of the essential building blocks of *Outliers* were simplistic and faulty. There was much quibbling over the 10,000-hour rule. In fact, Gladwell himself went on to say, "There is a lot of confusion about the ten-thousand-hour rule that I talk about in *Outliers*. . . . [P]ractice isn't a sufficient condition for success. I could play chess for one hundred years and I'll never be a grandmaster. The point is simply that natural ability requires a huge investment of time in order to be made manifest. . . . Achievement is talent plus preparation. . . . [T]he ten-thousand-hour research reminds us that 'the closer psychologists look at the careers of the gifted, the smaller the role innate talent seems to play and the bigger the role preparation seems to play.' In cognitively demanding fields, there are no naturals."[9]

Of course, politics is a demanding field. If a political leader performs poorly at something, like representing his or her

[6]Geoffrey Colvin, *Talent Is Overrated*, Portfolio, 2008, pp. 66–67.
[7]Ibid.
[8]Malcolm Gladwell, *Outliers*, Little, Brown and Company, 2008, p. 39.
[9]Malcom Gladwell, *Ask Me Anything on Reddit*, June 2, 2014.

state, that leader will likely fail to be reelected. Joe Biden performed well; he worked hard at his job. He certainly matched the 10,000-hour rule—and then some—to become the master politician he is. He was elected to the Senate in 1972 and every six years after that until he resigned from the Senate to become vice president in 2009. That made his résumé the most complete in Washington, D.C. Talent was not the only attribute that propelled him to the White House.

Be Authentic

One thing that friends, colleagues, and even acquaintances say about Joe Biden is that he is always himself. He is comfortable in his own skin. Perhaps his confidence emanates from the sum of his experiences and accomplishments. To help evaluate the experience in Joe Biden's portfolio, it is worth turning back the clock to when Barack Obama selected Biden as his vice president in 2008.

Before accepting the job as vice president, Biden told Obama, in a three-hour meeting at a low-key, Minneapolis hotel, that he would accept the post only if he could serve as a senior advisor. Biden told Obama he wanted to "be the last person in the room" before Obama pulled a trigger on a big decision. Obama agreed. Obama and Biden were mostly on the same page for the next eight years, in contrast to the preceding Democratic administration pairing of Bill Clinton and Al Gore, who did not like each other.

The main criteria for choosing a vice presidential candidate are, first, that he or she would be ready on day 1 to take over as president, and second, that he or she would be able to compensate for any weaknesses or "holes" in the presidential candidate's résumé. Joe Biden, the long-time politico, of course checked both boxes. Of most value was Biden's experience in foreign relations. Obama's opponent in 2008 was Senator John McCain, who had Biden-like foreign policy experience.

Biden was also selected for his humanity—for his empathy. When Biden was being considered for the number 2 post, Obama's senior aide and long-time friend David Axelrod visited with Biden at Biden's home in Delaware. The way Joe interacted so compassionately with his family touched Axelrod. He described Biden's disarming authenticity to the future president. He also told candidate Obama that there was something special about this man, alluding to Biden's humility.

Other distinguished individuals have recognized Joe Biden's authenticity. Political columnist and long-time Washington correspondent Jules Witcover wrote a biography of Biden a decade before Biden was elected president. Witcover concluded, "In writing the biography of Joe Biden a decade ago, I spent much time in Delaware asking locals across the state what they thought of him. I often raised his propensity for committing what were known as political gaffes in talking so much. The usual response, from admirers and critics alike, was the same: '*That's Joe.*' That is, Joe Biden was who he was: an open book who said what he thought when he thought it, letting the chips fall where they might."[10]

Witcover articulated Biden's authenticity: "In all his years in the Senate . . . and continuing to today, Joe Biden has thrived and survived politically and personally by being himself. At every turn, he pointedly has told his fellow Delawareans, and now the nation, that he gives them '*my word as a Biden,*' meaning they can take it to the bank."[11]

---

[10]Jules Witcover, "The Authentic Joe Biden," *Mining News*, December 5, 2020.
[11]Ibid.

Know That #2 Can Become an Effective #1

Earlier in the chapter, we identified the most common professional backgrounds and experience of the men elected to the presidency. Joe Biden's experience ostensibly surpasses every previous president. He was a practicing attorney for years, he participated in local politics for two years, he was a senator for 36 years, and he was the vice president from January 2009 to January 2017.

Is there any evidence that the 10,000-hour rule or 10-year rule (or whatever the number of thousands of hours are required) applies to presidential politics and, specifically, to Joe Biden becoming president? Based on Biden's political résumé, we can say that his eight years as vice president were the most relevant and most applicable of his career to prepare him for the presidency. Under the right circumstances, the role of vice president is the best, albeit imperfect, apprenticeship for the presidency.

If a president truly regards his vice president as a governing partner, he will be more likely to consult with her or him when weighing important legislative and other crucial matters. This approach to the vice presidency was not always in evidence. In the first years of the republic through much of the twentieth century, the vice presidency was viewed as a powerless position. One vice president, John Nance Garner who served under FDR, was not even trusted. He abhorred the number 2 job and opposed every piece of winning legislation put forth by Roosevelt. Nance Garner famously said the vice presidency was "not worth a bucket of warm piss."

In the past two decades, however, the vice presidency has become a far more prominent, muscular position. In recent administrations, presidents viewed their vice presidents as key advisors to help govern an increasingly complex nation and world. The vice president is also a member of the president's cabinet and serves on the National Security Council. And if the chemistry is right, the vice president can do more than advise. He or she can serve as a leadership partner and confidante.

For example, Vice President Biden played a decisive role in his negotiations with GOP members in Congress during both Obama terms. According to *Newsweek*, "[Biden] helped the Obama administration pass several key pieces of legislation, including the 2010 Tax Relief Act, the Budget Control Act of 2011, which dealt with a debt ceiling crisis, and the American Taxpayer Relief Act of 2012. The 2012 act resolved the so-called 'fiscal cliff.'"[12]

Newsweek also pointed to Biden's burden in getting the Affordable Care Act (ACA, or Obamacare) passed. The ACA will always be judged as Obama's cornerstone legislative accomplishment. Biden's role was viewed as keeping Democrats from jumping ship—a situation that would confront President Biden on numerous occasions. Obamacare passed in 2010 with almost no bipartisan support.

Commenting on Biden after he had served Obama for one term, James Traub, a columnist at *Foreign Policy,* stated, "It is safe to say that on foreign policy, Biden is the most powerful U.S. vice president in history save for his immediate predecessor, Dick Cheney." Traub described a White House in which Vice President Biden shaped the course of Obama's foreign relations: "Every morning that President Barack Obama chooses to receive the daily intelligence briefing in person,

---

[12]Darragh Roche, "What Joe Biden Has Achieved in 40 Years of Politics," *Newsweek*, October 22, 2020.

Vice President Joe Biden sits by his side in a matching armchair in the Oval Office. Biden attends—and often speaks volubly at—the 'Principals' meetings' of the president and his top national security officials, as well as at the president's weekly meetings with Secretary of State Hillary Clinton and Defense Secretary Leon Panetta."[13]

Traub's reporting also alluded to the friendship and respect the two men had for each other: "Often he [Biden] stays afterward for a few minutes of private talk, or the president walks over to Biden's office thirty paces down the hall. He and the president have lunch, by themselves, every week. In a White House where foreign policy is made, to an extraordinary extent, by the president and a few close advisors, Biden is first among equals."[14]

Two of Biden's greatest accomplishments as vice president fall under the umbrella of foreign policy and were widely noted and praised—specifically, the work he did on the Paris climate agreement and the Iran nuclear deal. The many hours he spent on foreign policy as vice president helped prepare him for his future role as president.

Do What It Takes to Be Persuasive

Some of the best research on leadership development has been conducted by John Zenger and Joseph Folkman.[15] They collected extensive data on what it takes to be perceived as a strong leader. After examining over 100,000 leadership

---

[13]James Traub, "The Biden Doctrine," *Foreign Policy*, October 10, 2012.
[14]Ibid.
[15]Full disclosure: I worked with John Zenger and Joseph Folkman and published the first edition of *The Extraordinary Leader* in 2002 as the business publisher of McGraw-Hill.

assessments, they concluded that it is nearly impossible to predict who will emerge as the most effective leaders: "There is clearly no one factor that anyone has identified that consistently predicts who will succeed as a leader."[16]

The Zenger/Folkman conclusion that no one can *predict* future leaders based on past assessments or glowing résumés appears to be at one end of the leadership research spectrum. At the opposite end is the Anders Ericsson/Colvin/Gladwell trio and the role of deliberate practice.

Predicting whether Joe Biden will be a great president based on his past is a fool's errand. The role of a leadership author should never be to delve into the predicting business. But when it comes to discussing and assessing the effectiveness of presidential leadership, the concepts of on-the-job training and deliberate practice have some usefulness.

The job of president is not a solo affair. It "takes a village" to run a country. But it falls most squarely on a president to get his or her legislative agenda approved by a co-equal branch of government. And it is not really one branch of government. For all practical purposes, Congress consists of two branches of government, the House and the Senate. Either chamber can kill any piece of agenda, no matter how noble the purpose of the proposed new law. That is always true but even more so when one branch of Congress is controlled by the opposing party (which, of course, was not true after Biden was elected).

The party that controls the White House usually loses seats in the mid-terms. For example, in the 2010 mid-terms, Obamacare was so unpopular that it resulted in a net loss of sixty-three Democratic seats in the House of Representatives, the most seats lost by either chamber of Congress since 1938.

[16]John Zenger and Joseph Folkman, *The New Extraordinary Leader*, 3d ed., McGraw-Hill, 2019, p. 178.

Biden similarly may find a far more difficult chess board in 2023 and thereafter.

Even if you control both chambers and the White House, there are lawmakers of every stripe who will oppose you. In other words, a Democratic president still has to worry about Democrats (e.g., Joe Manchin of West Virginia).

Lawmakers in either party might not like a given president and vote against the legislation because of personal reasons. And if it is not personal, they may be against what that leader is trying to accomplish. Even if they agree with proposed legislation, they may not vote for it. They may have a constituency back home that prefers a different outcome. In a situation like that, they may have to vote against their conscience if they want to keep their literal seats of power in their next primary or election.

To close the loop on Anders Ericsson's research, it is worth examining one key part of any manager's or president's job: *to persuade.* If one tried to reduce the entire world of a politician down to a single word, it would be *persuasion* (a word first used in the fourteenth century). The greatest politicians in American history knew extremely well how to persuade. They knew when to use the carrot and when to use the stick.

You do not have to be in politics to know that the ability to persuade through public speaking, private meetings, and phone calls is essential to success. Biden knew this. But, as he described during his 2020 presidential campaign, not only was he not a gifted speaker, but he also had an unforgettable stutter. He struggled with his speech impediment his entire life, and he still has one to this day.

Children can be cruel, as Biden learned early on. To overcome his disheartening stutter, he did two things: he practiced poetry for hours on end and, when he knew he was going to be called to say something in front of class, he practiced those words time and again under his breath until he committed those words to memory.

Biden's habit of practicing speeches continued for decades. His biographer Evan Osnos explained, "Unlike the greater Washington orators who inspired or surrounded him—John F. Kennedy, Daniel Patrick Moynihan, Bill Clinton, Barack Obama—Biden's was not a gift; it was a product of labor. Steve Solarz, the late New York congressman, once visited the Senate at night and found the chamber nearly empty. 'There was one person on the floor, orating as though it were the Roman Colosseum, and it was Joe Biden.'"[17]

While the 10,000-hour rule may have some limits, Joe Biden showed what it took to get past something he expected would plague him his entire life. Speaking became a dominant part of the Biden business. He practiced speaking more than most any of his peers. He practiced out of sight and under his breath. He worked harder than anyone to correct his speech so that he could persuade. His perseverance paid off in the end.

Learn from Your Worst Experiences

In June 1987, a decade-and-a-half after serving in the Senate, Joe Biden announced his first of three runs for the presidency. At the time, the favorite son of Delaware was viewed as a fresh face with a promising, blue-sky future. Unfortunately, things did not turn out well.

Several months earlier, Biden decided to try some themes and biographical stories in his speeches. The only problem was that his speeches contained facts and features from *other*

---

[17]Evan Osnos, *Joe Biden: The Life, the Run, and What Matters Now*, Scribner, 2020, p. 33.

people's lives. Here is how the *New York Times* described one early event from the 1988 campaign: " 'When I marched in the civil rights movement, I did not march with a 12-point program,' Biden thundered, testing his presidential message in February 1987 before a New Hampshire audience. 'I marched with tens of thousands of others to change attitudes. And we changed attitudes.'"[18]

As his staff reminded Joe Biden, he did not march in the civil rights movement. Did the candidate alter his approach after being prodded by his team? Biden told his staff that he understood the problem, and then he kept exaggerating and lying.

Making up stories that never happened was not his biggest problem. Plagiarism was. From his days back in law school through the 2020 campaign, more than 50 years combined, Joe Biden inexplicably made the same mistake over and over. Let us examine these missteps in chronological order.

While a student at Syracuse University Law School, Biden turned in a law review paper without properly citing five pages of his work. There were no quotation marks or source citations that would have aided Biden's efforts to minimize the transgression. The punishment seemed light: Biden was not suspended or expelled. He just had to repeat the course.

If that was the extent of Biden's plagiaristic ways, history might have turned out differently. Alas, it was not.

In 1987, in his first of three attempts at the presidency, Biden made several claims about his résumé that were untrue; in addition, he plagiarized a British leader's speech without attribution. The speech was delivered by Biden at the Iowa State Fair. Biden had plagiarized "several portions" from Neil

[18]Matt Flegenheimer, "Biden's First Run for Presidency Was a Calamity," *New York Times*, June 3, 2019.

Kinnock, a member of the British Labor Party and member of Parliament from 1970 to 1995. Once word got out about the stolen passages of the speech, the press dug deeper. In a short time, they discovered what Biden had perpetrated in law school.

All the awful press drowned out any other message, and Joe Biden had to withdraw from the race in about 90 days after he announced his entrance to the race. "I made some mistakes," Joe Biden explained to the press in September 1987. "But now, the exaggerated shadow of those mistakes has begun to obscure the essence of my candidacy and the essence of Joe Biden."[19]

That statement suggests that Biden understood his own self-destructive ways. However, Biden struggled to control or deal effectively with the subject of his plagiarism. One of the mysteries associated with the mistakes he made in his first and later second presidential runs was that Biden had such a vivid and compelling story to tell as tragic as it was. He had no need to bolster his record with lies or lift excerpts of speeches from other politicians.

Biden's biographer put forth his theory of what caused Biden to repeat the same error time and again: "Looking over the record of his exaggerations and plagiarism, I came to see them as the excesses of a man who wanted every story to sing . . . . [E]ven at the risk of embarrassment . . . the costs of that weakness have been steep, but Biden only fitfully acknowledged them."[20]

There is one other thought on Biden's penchant for plagiarizing. It is put forward here (by this author) because of its simplicity: What if Joe Biden was simply lazy? That makes

---

[19]Joe Biden, Campaign Withdrawal Speech, September 24, 1987.
[20]Evan Osnos, *Joe Biden: The Life, the Run, and What Matters Now*, Scribner, 2020, p. 47.

more sense than, say, he was dishonest. Besides the plagiarizing, there are few cases of Joe Biden openly, knowingly lying to anyone. Even the British politician whose speech he borrowed, Neil Kinnock, felt strongly and said in 2020 that Joe is "an honest man."

When given a chance to comment on his first bid for president, there was a complete absence of bravado from Biden's response. Instead, he demonstrated that he had finally come to terms with what he had done: "I made a mistake, and it was born out of my arrogance. I didn't deserve to be president."[21]

What's the Takeaway?

- **Understand the Value of Experience**. Biden's half a century of political leadership made him uniquely qualified to follow the least experienced U.S. president. If you have a skill, trade or profession you love, then you may just need to put in more than 10,000 hours of deliberate practice to enter the stratosphere of your chosen fields.

- **Develop Your *Greatest* Strengths**. The Zenger/Folkman research proved that the key to being perceived as a strong leader center around developing just a few strengths. However, these strengths must really shine. Being a great speaker is helpful and a key strength, so if you are good at that, find venues to speak as often as possible to further enhance that strength. The same applies to other strengths, such as excelling at client relationships.

[21]Joe Biden, Interview, NPR, August 1, 2007.

- **Take Immediate Responsibility When Things Go Wrong.** The Afghanistan maelstrom was Joe Biden's responsibility. President Biden needed to apologize for the botched evacuation immediately, then pivoted to describe all the steps he and his key cabinet members were taking to help improve the situation. Biden, however, should be credited with airlifting over 125,000 Afghans and Americans out of the country, the largest civilian airlift in history.

CHAPTER 4

Build on Strengths

When we build on our strengths and daily successes—instead of focusing on failures—we simply learn more.

—Tom Rath

The importance of the mindset of a leader cannot be overestimated, especially when it comes to the highest job in the land. Every move and utterance of an American president is closely watched by people and the press in America and across the globe.

The best leaders are optimistic by nature. They see possibilities in valuing life and leading by example and want their fellow citizens to flourish and prosper.

At its heart, leadership is, of course, about people. And when you get right down to its roots, leadership can only grow and prosper when it is grounded in decency. Decency, ethics, and humility—these "soft" virtues are considered areas of strength for President Biden. Perhaps surprisingly, he was not always perceived as strong in these areas.

Take 1991 and his handling of the Anita Hill hearings, when Biden was chair of the Judiciary Committee. Biden treated Hill with tremendous disrespect. He did not acknowledge her bravery in telling her story when she had so little to gain and so much to lose in challenging Clarence Thomas on his nomination to the U.S. Supreme Court. This event took place 30 years before Biden became president and about 25 years prior to the still-going-strong "me-too" movement.

People often take decades to self-actualize and maximize their perceived strengths. How did Joe Biden go from the man he was in 1991 to the man he is today? Many analysts would suggest that Biden's growth came about by enhancing his strengths and not focusing on his weaknesses.

The first management theorist to focus on the importance of building strengths was Peter Drucker. In 1967, in his groundbreaking book *The Effective Executive*, he wrote this gem, dozens of years ahead of his time: "The effective executive makes strengths productive. To achieve results, one [must] use all the available strengths—the strengths of associates, the strength of the superior, and one's own strengths. These strengths are the true opportunities. To make strength productive is the unique purpose of the organization. It cannot overcome the weaknesses with which each of us is endowed, but it can make them irrelevant."[1]

In the 1990s and more prominently in the 2000s, this "new" strand of leadership emerged as one of the best things in business thinking. Based on their landmark, 30-year, 2 million–person study, Don Clifton and the Gallup Organization published a book entitled *Now Discover Your Strengths*. That book and a later sequel, *Strengths Finder 2.0* by Tom Rath, sparked and undergirded this new and burgeoning field.

Strengths-based training swept through corporate America like a house on fire. Millions of managers were learning the importance of bolstering strengths rather than fixing "irrelevant" weaknesses. A "strengths mindset" is as important in the world of government as it is in business. By focusing on what they already do well, political leaders among others give themselves a chance for their best assets to shine while keeping insignificant weaknesses insignificant.

---

[1]Peter F. Drucker, *The Effective Executive*, 1967.

Be Curious and Read Everything

President Biden has shown that he understands the cost of admission to his lofty environs at 1600 Pennsylvania Avenue. He is, and has been, responsible for his own leadership development. He did not inherit a great name, just an honest one. He earned each mile along his route to becoming a prepared statesman and skilled legislator.

Biden knew that to excel at being president he would need to "up his game." An inquisitive person by nature, Biden is an avid reader of books, magazines, papers, intelligence briefings, and daily briefings. His curiosity and reading habits are both key strengths for a U.S. president, who can, on rare occasions, shift the course of history with one new, big idea.

Biden prefers to read about big ideas—to read well-regarded books that describe American exceptionalism. One such example is historian Jon Meacham's *Soul of America: The Battle for Our Better Angels* (2018). Meacham's themes dovetail nicely with Biden's own thoughts of democracy, which explains, in part, why Biden and Meacham became friends. (It better explains why Biden used Meacham to write some of his speeches before disclosing that fact publicly.)

Another Biden favorite is Jonathan Alter's *The Defining Moment: FDR's Hundred Days and the Triumph of Hope* (2006), which describes in detail Franklin Roosevelt's first 100 days in office. Biden's great takeaway from that book? Democracies are not permanent fixtures, a vital lesson for any U.S. president in a post–January 6, 2021 (when rioters stormed the U.S. Capitol building) world.

In an interview with podcast creator Brené Brown, Biden, building on his reading, reflected on American democracy: "There's no such factor as an assured democracy. It has to be fought for each time. If you read just the first chapter [of Alter's book] . . . guys like [political reporter] Walter Lippmann were telling Roosevelt, 'We have to have a dictatorship to get it right.' . . . There's nothing automatic about this. We've got to earn it every single generation. And I used to hear that all the time and think, 'That's not true. We have it permanently.' No, see what's happening now?"[2] On January 6, 2021, America entered an era of polarization not seen since the 1960s, and President Biden was attempting to ring the bell in the town square to alert as many of his fellow citizens as possible.

Biden's acknowledgment that democracies are fragile takes on an outsized proportion in these turbulent, sometimes terrifying, times. The concept harkens back to Benjamin Franklin and the Constitutional Convention in 1787. Upon leaving Independence Hall in Philadelphia, Franklin was queried: "What kind of government do we have?" "*A Republic,*" he said, adding this wise caveat: "*if you can keep it.*" (That story is also a favorite of House Leader Nancy Pelosi, who quoted it often before Biden became president.)

A clear understanding of the American experiment, which turned into spectacle in the opening decades of the twenty-first century, is what separates President Biden from many of his predecessors. He sees things as they are, with clear eyes and a vast knowledge of U.S. history and the American ideal. He has positioned himself well as the leader of the free world.

Reach Across the Aisle

When he ran for the presidency, Biden touted his ability to get things done "across the aisle" as one of his greatest strengths.

---

[2]Joe Biden, Interview, Brené Brown Podcast, June 20, 2021.

He did not believe in throwing any shade at the Republican party. That was contrary to who he was. He almost always described members of the GOP as "my Republican friends." He spent half his life in the Senate. Many of these lawmakers were his friends.

He not only promised he would reach across the aisle, but also vowed to get things done on behalf of the American people. Most every president makes promises about their cross-party, vote-getting potential, but few ever deliver. President Biden is turning out to be the deliverer-in-chief.

His $1.9 trillion Covid-19 relief bill was followed by two infrastructure bills—the pair totaling a near $5 trillion in assistance for the lower and middle classes.[3] Biden pulled off what the *Washington Post* called a "political miracle": the "smaller" $1.2 trillion bill was passed with bipartisan support by the Senate on August 10, 2021, with full expectation that it will pass the House. Nineteen senators, including Minority Leader Mitch McConnell, crossed over to vote with Democrats on the largest infrastructure bill in history.

Prior to the vote, every soothsayer and naysayer in the country said it could not be done. Bipartisanship is a relic of a bygone era, they argued. The ink on a functioning two-party-system obituary has long since dried, claimed most in the media. Nonetheless, with that vote in the stormy days of August 2021, Joe Biden made good on his promise to reach agreement with his "Republican friends" across the aisle. And he did it all with dignity, boldness, and empathy. That's the Joe Biden way. He checks emotions and as many biases as possible

---

[3]At the time this book was completed, the $1.2 trillion bipartisan infrastructure bill was passed in the Senate and headed to the House for its vote after the August 2021 recess. Gaining passage in the Senate with 69 votes was a near unheard of event in the previous dozen years under both Democratic and Republican presidents.

at the door of the Oval Office. He then works tirelessly behind the scenes to come up with what he views as big solutions for big problems.

He was not always like that, as we saw in the previous chapter when he repeatedly took the words and ideas of others and presented them as his own. But that was not *this* Joe Biden—the Joe Biden of 2021. Like the best among us, he had matured, evolved, and self-actualized over the years and decades.

Leaders must be right for the times in which they are beckoned to lead. The right leader at the wrong time is doomed to failure. The 29-year-old lawyer who defeated a sure-to-win incumbent Delaware senator named Caleb Boggs in 1971—plus 50 years—is the right man for his time. He is such a man because of who he has become, what he values, and the deep emotional pain he has endured in his life. His years in the Senate and the tragic realities he suffered made him an absolute realist about life, America, and the world. He needed that clear-eyed vision to assess the political situation and "face reality."

The August 2021 Senate vote on infrastructure was a seminal event in the presidency of Joe Biden. Nineteen senators voted in lockstep on a record infrastructure bill. There were few, if any, who could remember the last time something like that took place in the well of the United States Senate.

"This historic investment in infrastructure is what I believe you, the American people, want, what you've been asking for for a long, long time," extolled Biden. In the same White House statement, Biden thanked Republicans for exhibiting "a lot of courage."[4]

"I was proud to support today's historic bipartisan infrastructure deal and prove that both sides of the political aisle

---

[4]Joe Biden, Statement, The White House, August 10, 2021.

can still come together around common-sense solutions," declared minority leader Mitch McConnell.[5] McConnell had voted for a record-setting Democratic, Biden bill. Hell had finally frozen over.

Don't Forget Culture or People

In the last chapter we explored Joe Biden's decades of experience in the Senate and eight years as vice president, both of which consisted of over 10,000 hours of work. It is no accident that the ideas in this chapter—how leaders build on strengths—follows the part of the book that demonstrates the unique roles of practice and experience in determining great mastery of a skill or profession.

While it is easy to total years on a résumé, it is less easy to quantify the strengths Biden brought to each of these posts, as well as the strengths that he acquired during the years of experience performing these important jobs. And while it cannot be quantified, it is worth trying to figure out what each of Biden's two major political positions (senator and vice president) contributed to his readiness for the office at 1600 Pennsylvania Avenue.

Joe Biden executes successfully because he developed and honed a canny knack of what it takes to succeed inside the Beltway. He learned the difference between an ally and a foe and the shades of gray that separated the two. That ability derived from his decades serving as the senior senator from Delaware. He knew where the bodies were buried, dead or alive (some senators are dead but do not know it yet).

---

[5]Mitch McConnell, Press Statement, Mitch McConnell Republican Leader, August 10, 2021.

The Senate has been called "the most deliberative body in the world." The only problem, says the *Washington Examiner*, is "that it no longer deliberates."[6] It did deliberate, however, during Joe Biden's tenure in the Senate. And he was one of the most prominent "deliberators."

Nonetheless, time serving in those sacred halls provides only a part of a politician's political acumen. It is usually the informal parts of their lives, often on the fringes of their workdays, that inform their opinions, attitudes, and actions. Senators are people, too, and they generally adhere to some set of norms just like any other group. Senators interact with each other in the back rooms and halls and offices of the Senate, in apartments, over drinks, at dinners, at hotels, and while traveling around the world. Decades of these interactions give senators a deep understanding of the inner-beltway-of-life.

In both government and business, the culture of an institution or a nation is often the most overlooked or neglected by its leaders. Understanding the culture of an institution as complex as the U.S. Senate is critical to success within that institution. Interestingly, what rankles many senior senators are the freshly minted men and women who show up on day one ready to change an institution or set of norms they do not fully comprehend.

One of Joe Biden's strengths was his deep knowledge of the stark reality and deeply troubled "culture" he would inherit upon entering the Oval Office. Hate was thriving. Things like anti-Semitism and violence against Asians were soaring. Joe Biden understood the malignant culture that permeated the previous administration and voiced his desire for

[6]David Davenport, " 'It Sucks': The Senate, the World's Greatest Deliberative Body, No Longer Deliberates," *Washington Examiner*, April 2, 2018.

him and his team to be perceived as the opposite. That meant modeling positive behavior every day. To really hit the ground running, however, he had to start months before taking the oath of office.

When people think of great leaders, they associate them through a lens of actions and accomplishment—and the steps taken to achieve or surpass some important goal, fight through an obstacle, or overcome a series of challenges. In short, effective execution almost always calls on a leader to rely on his or her own strengths to reach some literal or figurative finish line.

During the presidential transition and the first weeks and months on the job, the president-elect makes a series of decisions that makes the difference between success and failure in an administration: he selects his cabinet and other key members of the team that he will count on to help him get his agenda accomplished.

The same is true in organizations of all stripes, big and small. In any organization, the person at the top communicates direction, articulates a mission, and espouses company values, among many other things. However, obviously he or she cannot be expected to handle everything. Most tasks must be performed by others.

Jim Collins, author of the iconic book *Good to Great* (2001), explained that it was getting the right people on board that counted as the most determining variable of success in any organization: "The good-to-great leaders understood three important truths. First, with the right people, your organization or unit will be more able to change with a changing world. They will be able to course correct far more effectively than a weak team. Second, if you have the right people on the bus, the problems on how to manage and motivate people largely goes away. Third, with the wrong people, it doesn't matter if you have the other parts right—like strategy and direction—you still won't have a great company."[7]

From his earliest days in office, President Biden proved he understood the absolute primacy of the team over the individual. Unlike his predecessor, Biden made it crystal clear that he wanted a cabinet that prayed at the altar of the Constitution, not at the altar of himself.

Build Multiple Strengths to Become Extraordinary

In the last chapter, I introduced two leadership experts whose work has been celebrated, time-tested, and beyond reproach: John Zenger and Joseph Folkman. They are the authors of *The New Extraordinary Leader* (2019),[8] where they make one of the most convincing arguments—backed by a fortress of research—that the best, most capable leaders are those that are perceived to possess *multiple strengths*. Zenger and Folkman demonstrated that having two or three strengths can make a huge difference in how one is perceived as a leader.

In *How to Be Exceptional* (2012), a four-author team led by Zenger made an extraordinary display of the power of building on strengths. They chose two specific strengths—having "technical or professional expertise" and "communicates powerfully and prolifically." They then revealed that a leader who possesses both of those strengths will be perceived as a strong leader by 82 percent of people rather than less than 15 percent if a leader had only one of the two characteristics.

---

[7]Jim Collins, *Good to Great*, Harper Business, 2001, p. 42.
[8]Full disclosure: I was the acquisitions editor/publisher for the first edition of this book.

Put another way, having a combination of strengths and competencies is the key to being a strong leader: "Technical expertise without powerful communications is much like a great professor who teaches as a mime would."[9]

Joe Biden has spent the entirety of his career developing multiple key strengths, in particular, expertise in both domestic and foreign policy along with strong communication skills. He leads with empathy and he knows of what he speaks. This combination of skills is a powerful one indeed.

Ultimately, Zenger and Folkman contended that there was an even more pivotal form of leadership than action alone: "The highest expression of leadership involves change . . . through a new strategic direction, changing culture, or changing the fundamental business model. Thus, change is an important and ultimate criterion by which to measure leadership effectiveness."[10] As we shall see in his dealings with Russia, Biden was willing to invoke change as well.

Call Out Your Antagonists

As we know, one of President Biden's great strengths is his deep knowledge of foreign affairs, policy, and world leaders. That knowledge was acquired and honed on half a century's worth of experience, especially as a member and three-time chair of the prestigious Foreign Relation Committee.

Prior to becoming vice president in 2009, Biden already had traveled the world and met with dozens of world leaders.

---

[9]John Zenger, Joseph Folkman, Robert Sherwin, and Barbara Steel, *How to Be Exceptional: Drive Leadership Success by Magnifying Your Strengths,* McGraw-Hill, 2012.
[10]John Zenger and Joseph Folkman, *The New Extraordinary Leader*, 3d ed., McGraw-Hill, 2020, p. 19.

He also held scores of hearings on foreign affairs, issues, and policies. He was widely regarded as one of America's best foreign relations expert politicians, which explains, in no small measure, why one-term Senator Barack Obama selected him as his vice presidential running mate in 2008 (Obama did not have experience on the international front).

Biden's expertise would be needed in dealing with Russia three decades after the end of the Cold War. Biden's four predecessors—Bill Clinton, George W. Bush, Barack Obama, and Donald Trump—had all been played, or at least outplayed, by Russian President Vladimir Putin, the former KGB officer and spy. All four thought they could reinvigorate U.S./Russian relations by appeasing Putin. They were wrong. They each showed naïveté in their dealings with him.[11]

Joe Biden had different plans. Early on in his administration, he let it be known that he had no qualms about taking a hard stance with Vladimir Putin. In an interview with George Stephanopoulos, Biden discussed his "long conversation" with the Russian dictator. He said that Russia would suffer consequences for its actions if it was confirmed beyond doubt that Russia had interfered with the 2020 U.S. elections. In the same interview, Biden called Vladimir Putin "a killer . . . having no soul."[12]

According to Biden's recollection of his own experience as vice president, Biden told Putin that when he looked in Putin's eyes, Biden saw "no soul." After being called "soulless," Putin responded slyly to Biden: "Then we understand one other."[13]

---

[11]Vladimir Putin assumed leadership upon Boris Yeltsin's surprise resignation on December 31, 1999. President Bill Clinton was the first to meet with Putin just a few months after Putin became the Russian president. Putin did not take Clinton seriously in 2000 as he viewed Clinton as a lame duck.

[12]Joe Biden, Interview with George Stephanopoulos, ABC News, *Good Morning America*, March 17, 2021.

[13]Ibid.

Biden's frank talk with George Stephanopolous signaled the quickest, most head-spinning reversal in U.S. approach, attitude, and policy toward another superpower in more than a generation. Unlike his predecessors, Joe Biden, secure in the knowledge of American exceptionalism, American strength, and the democratic way of life, was not going to tolerate the offensive, aggressive actions of Putin and Russia.

A thug like Putin was ill-accustomed to being called a killer by a sitting U.S. president—and not quietly, but in an ABC News interview that would be repeated on scores of international cable news networks and disseminated across every social media platform in the world. As a result, unsurprisingly, Putin was furious with Joe Biden.

No one could remember any president (or secretary of state) speaking out so publicly against Vladimir Putin (well, Hillary Clinton did half of that and earned twice Putin's ire, ending in the election of Donald Trump over her). Experts agree that Barack Obama was too lax with Putin. According to the Brookings Institution, "We should not slip into collective amnesia over the Obama administration's weak and underwhelming response to Russian aggression. Throughout his presidency, Obama consistently underestimated the challenge posed by Putin's regime. . . . [Obama's] foreign policy was firmly grounded in the premise that Russia was not a national security threat to the United States. In 2012, Obama disparaged Mitt Romney for exaggerating the Russian threat—'the 1980s are now calling to ask for their foreign policy back because the Cold War's been over for 20 years,' Obama quipped. This breezy attitude prevailed even as Russia annexed Crimea, invaded eastern Ukraine, intervened in Syria, and hacked the Clinton campaign and the DNC."[14]

[14]Benjamin Haddad and Alina Polyakova, Brookings Institution, *Don't Rehabilitate Obama on Russia*, March 5, 2018.

Fast-forward a decade and the Biden accusation seemed to stun Putin, like a boxer who gets surprised by an unexpectedly strong left hook. In highly unusual fashion, in response to an accusation that apparently hit too close to home, Putin made a series of unusual, erratic steps.

First, Putin recalled his Russian ambassador from the United States "for consultations." Recalling an ambassador to his native country is a serious decision, one that Russia had not taken in more than two decades. The Russian foreign minister released a statement calling for the end of a "deterioration in relations" between the United States and Russia: "The most important thing for us is to identify ways of rectifying Russia-US relations, which have been going through hard times as Washington has, as a matter of fact, brought them to a blind alley. We are interested in preventing an irreversible deterioration in relations, if the Americans become aware of the risks associated with this."[15]

Second, when asked about the accusation that he was a murderer, Putin responded that he wished nothing but "good health" to the American president, "without irony or jokes." That statement left some to wonder if that was some veiled threat. But Putin's remarks continued. He taunted Biden, as a schoolyard bully might, by chiding him. He said, loosely translated, that it takes one to know one (meaning it takes a killer to know a killer).

Then to finish his confused trifecta, on the same day that Putin (may have) threatened Biden, Putin turned around and invited Biden to "Zoom talks." The three steps seemed incongruous and confusing. It was as if Vladimir Putin was so surprised by the all-so-public accusation that he had no idea what to do. Biden won round one with Putin, but truth be told, no one seemed to notice.

---

[15]Maria Zakharova, Press Release, The Ministry of Foreign Affairs of the Russian Federation, March 17, 2021.

Be Tough but Proportional

One of Biden's great strengths as president is his strong penchant to keep his word whenever humanly possible. No one can keep every promise, but he certainly kept most and performed beyond expectations. In the George Stephanopolous interview with ABC News, Biden said he would issue tough sanctions on Russia if his people assured him that Russia again interfered with the 2020 elections (which Biden knew it did).

The *Chicago Tribune* reminded us that Biden had been tough on Russia for most of the previous 15 years: "Since leaving office in 2017 [as Vice President], Biden sharpened his criticism of Russia. Months after leaving office, he penned a major article detailing Putin's 'assault on democracy' and the need to fight back. During the presidential campaign he frequently called Putin and his regime 'KGB thugs' and declared that Russia was 'the biggest threat to America.'"[16]

On April 15, 2021, Biden made good on his promise to sanction Vladimir Putin's Russia. Biden had forewarned the Russian leader days earlier in a "candid and respectful conversation." In making his announcement of sanctions, Biden said, "Today, I've approved several steps, including expulsion of several Russian officials, as a consequence of their actions. I've also signed an executive order authorizing new measures, including sanctions to address specific harmful actions that Russia has taken against U.S. interests. I was clear with President Putin that we could have gone further, but I chose not to do so, to be—I chose to be proportionate."[17]

---

[16]Ivo Daalder, "Biden, Who Has Been Around the Block with Putin," *Chicago Tribune*, January 28, 2021.
[17]Joe Biden, Statement, The White House, April 15, 2021.

Ultimately, the American president sanctioned 38 individuals and entities for election interference. He sanctioned eight individuals and entities for the invasion of Crimea. He also expelled 10 Russian diplomats from the United States. However, said Biden, he was not looking to start a war, cold or otherwise, with Russia.

Here is how Joe Biden explained his actions: "The United States is not looking to kick off a cycle—of escalation and conflict with Russia. We want a stable, predictable relationship. If Russia continues to interfere with our democracy, I'm prepared to take further actions to respond. It is my responsibility, as President of the United States, to do so. But throughout our long history of competition, our two countries have been able to find ways to manage tensions and to keep them from escalating out of control. . . . When I spoke to President Putin, I expressed my belief that communication between the two of us, personally and directly, was to be essential in moving forward to a more effective relationship. And he agreed on that point. . . . Now is the time to de-escalate. The way forward is through thoughtful dialogue and diplomatic process. The U.S. is prepared to continue constructively to move forward that process. My bottom line is this: Where it is in the interest of the United States to work with Russia, we should and we will. Where Russia seeks to violate the interests of the United States, we will respond. And we'll always stand in defense of our country, our institutions, our people, and our allies."[18]

Be Attentive to Leadership Blind Spots

The worst day of the early Biden presidency occurred in his eighth month in office. Mayhem ensued in Afghanistan after

[18]Ibid.

President Biden pulled American troops out of the country as he and his predecessor had promised.[19]

The problem wasn't necessarily pulling the troops. The disaster was that Biden pulled them out too quickly, risking the lives of thousands of Americans and Afghans.

No one thought that the Afghan forces would collapse so quickly. Some reports predicted it would take perhaps 90 days for the Taliban to take control of Kabul. It happened in 90 *hours*.

This was a humanitarian disaster, a breakdown of intelligence, and a failure of leadership, and not in that order. The gut-wrenching scene of many hundreds of Afghans running after U.S. military aircraft, some clutching to the hot metal of the fuselage as the plane took off, was all caught on camera and broadcast around the world.

This entire woeful episode ending America's longest war provokes the following key question: What do you do when a perceived strength turns into an apparent weakness? Joe Biden was the foreign relations expert of his day. That was how he positioned himself in his presidential campaign. It was meant to be one of his great strengths.

But President Biden made a significant mistake in execution of a foreign policy objective. We may never know how costly this mistake was, but we can learn lessons from how he handled things after the horrific scenes were broadcast across the country and the world.

Timely communication is a must in addressing a dire and complex situation gone bad. Twenty-four hours after

---

[19]In February 2020 the United States and the Taliban entered an accord entitled, ironically, "Agreement for Bringing Peace to Afghanistan." That document included a stipulation for all American and NATO forces to leave Afghanistan in stages, with all gone by May 1, 2021. Biden moved the date to September 11, 2021. In July, Biden moved the date to August 31, 2021.

the Taliban took the capital of Kabul, Biden spoke to the American people. His remarks were candid, but they fell short. Effective brinkmanship and political dogma say that if you are explaining, you're losing, and Biden was explaining day after day. Here is an example from one such White House speech: "And here's what I believe to my core: It is wrong to order American troops to step up when Afghanistan's own armed forces would not. If the political leaders of Afghanistan were unable to come together for the good of their people . . . they would never have done so while U.S. troops remained in Afghanistan bearing the brunt of the fighting for them."[20]

Let us back up a bit to emphasize what went wrong. It was not the decision to exit Afghanistan that was the mistake. It was the flawed *execution* of the decision Biden inherited and agreed with—the evacuation of thousands of Americans and the Afghan allies who helped American service men and women (those Afghans were vetted for, and received, special immigrant visas).

Later in that same White House speech, Biden proved he had buried the lead when he said this: "I am President of the United States of America, and the buck stops with me." Biden needed to turn that speech upside down and take responsibility for the blunder straight away. Simply stating the right words after making excuses and delivering lengthy explanations was not an acceptable response.

Leaders will be forgiven a mistake if they take responsibility and are perceived as being completely earnest and transparent in their apology. That will help reestablish trust and form a foundation to turn the situation around. In addition, swift action needs to be taken by the leader to make things

[20]Joe Biden, Remarks, The White House, August 16, 2021.

right—to right the ship that has recently touched and dotted the shoals.

For Biden, immediately ordering in thousands of more troops to deal with a substantial evacuation was necessary. The numbers told of the daunting nature of the task ahead. It fell to Biden to evacuate between 5,000 and 10,000 American citizens, as well as tens of thousands of Afghan interpreters. Within 96 hours, President Biden ordered in 8,000 troops, including three battalions of the Army's 82nd Airborne Division. Biden also said he would stay past August 31 if the situation required it. But the damage had been done.

In the short term, did Biden learn his lesson? Probably not.

Even after the world witnessed the worst scenes in Kabul, after it was apparent that the chaos could have been mitigated with more competent planning, Biden hoped to stop the political bleeding by granting a major television network interview. Biden was asked by ABC News's George Stephanopoulos, "You don't think this exit could have been handled any better in any way . . . [that you made] no mistakes?" President Biden stuttered a bit, then said sharply, "No. I don't think it could have been. . . . [T]he idea that somehow there's a way to have gotten out without chaos ensuing, I don't know how that happens."[21] Really?

One of Biden's problems was that on at least three occasions he promised a smoother transition in America's withdrawal from Afghanistan. After the ABC News interview, it was clear that Biden had a blind spot brought on by an outsized ego (no one reaches the Oval Office without one). Most every U.S. president has had a leadership blind spot of one kind or another. The sheer number of presidents to suffer from this malady, however, does not absolve Biden of his

[21]Joe Biden, Interview with George Stephanopoulos, ABC News, August 19, 2021.

responsibility to get important things right; nor does it excuse careless planning. Time, events, and history will judge how much Biden's blind spot will undermine his effectiveness.

What's the Takeaway?

- **Focus On Strengths, Not Weaknesses.** As the research in this chapter revealed, the key to leadership development lies in one's ability to set aside petty weaknesses. The great leaders often have amazing strengths. FDR used the radio to exhibit one of his greatest strengths, empathy. Joe Biden has the same empathy gene as the most effective leaders.

- **Develop Your *Greatest* Strengths.** The Zenger/Folkman research proved that the key to being perceived as a strong leader centers around developing just a few strengths. However, these strengths must really shine. Being a great speaker is helpful and a key strength, so if you are good at that, find venues to speak as often as possible to further enhance that strength. The same applies to other strengths, such as excelling at client relationships.

- **Take Immediate Responsibility When Things Go Wrong.** The Afghanistan maelstrom was Joe Biden's responsibility. President Biden needed to apologize for the botched evacuation immediately, then pivoted to describe all the steps he and his key cabinet members were taking to help improve the situation. Biden, however, should be credited with airlifting over 125,000 Afghans and Americans out of the country, the largest civilian airlift in history.

CHAPTER 5

Close Reality Gaps

The evacuation of thousands of people from Kabul is going to be hard and painful.

—Joe Biden

The world watched the chaos in Kabul, Afghanistan, as President Biden acknowledged the enormity of the task of evacuating American citizens and allies, but not his role in miscalculating what played out for the world to see. Biden never acknowledged the obvious reality that he could have called for Americans and our Afghan allies to leave that country weeks, even months, before the country collapsed to the Taliban in mid-August 2021.

In the waning days of America's longest war, the president had no choice but to proceed with great urgency amid widespread criticism. He did not, however, admit an error in judgment, creating a "reality gap." Reality gaps have the potential to behave like booby traps, small bombs, that can blow up in a leader's face at any time. Creating a reality gap is ill-advised, much the same as being unaware of blind spots, as discussed earlier.

Make Good on Your Promises Even in the Face of Crisis

Whether it was bad intelligence or miscalculation, the chaotic and uncoordinated pullout from Afghanistan will always be seen as a failure by President Biden and his administration.

Nonetheless, Biden remained undeterred in setting things right. His actions in Afghanistan were swift. As soon as the Kabul airport bottleneck became apparent, Biden hit the accelerator, moving with unprecedented speed to step up efforts to evacuate Americans and Afghans from Kabul and the rest of the country. Biden left no stone unturned to get people out.

The United States was getting help from veteran organizations, veterans, and groups in an aptly titled "Digital Dunkirk." One such participating officer, Charlie Reeder, served two tours in Afghanistan and explained part of the epic effort: "We are a collection of veterans, civilians, people in the military and defense agencies around the world that are trying to get as many of the interpreters and those who have helped us . . . in Afghanistan out as soon as possible. And we've been coordinating between each group . . . or just trying to push as hard as we can to get that paperwork through and approved by the State Department."[1]

Biden ordered six airlines to help with the evacuations from "secondary" or "third party" locations, only the third time in history the Civil Reserve Air Fleet had been activated. He also ordered that Americans be airlifted by choppers from various checkpoints to the Hamid Karzei Airport.

The United States was able to evacuate more than 10,000 Americans and Afghans with special immigrant visas (SIVs) within a 24-hour period, two days in a row as well as 20,000 evacuees in one 24-hour span. In one 10-day period, the United States was able to airlift 70,000 Americans, allies, and Afghans. For several days in succession, at its peak, incredibly, a plane took off from the Kabul airport every 39 minutes.

---

[1]"Digital Dunkirk," Yahoo Finance, August 24, 2021.

Overall, more than 125,000 Americans, Afghans, allies, and asylum seekers were saved from Afghanistan during the evacuation. About two-thirds were evacuated by the U.S. military and a third by America's coalition partners. It was the largest, most sweeping civilian airlift in history.

The president gave daily briefings on the evacuation. Biden's empathetic third speech on the topic closer resembled the reality on the ground, helping Biden close the reality gap: "The evacuation of thousands of people from Kabul is going to be hard and painful. . . . There is no way to evacuate this many people without pain and loss and the heartbreaking images you see on television. . . . My heart aches for those people you see. We have proven we can move thousands of people a day out of Kabul . . . but we have a long way to go, and a lot can still go wrong."[2]

The Taliban had vowed to the United States that they would safeguard Americans and aid their departure. Unfortunately, the armed gunmen, little more than thugs, had zero experience in controlling any perimeters and at best acted as crowd controllers.

Biden warned for several days of credible, potentially imminent, threats against the Hamid Karzei Airport. His words were prescient. With only several days to go before his evacuation deadline of August 31, a suicide bomb went off on August 26 at the Abbey Gate of the airport, where more than a dozen American service people were among the many hundreds of Afghans assembled.

The terrorist group responsible for the attack was ISIS-K (meaning ISIS in Khorasan). Thirteen U.S. service members were killed and an additional eighteen were wounded. More than 170 Afghan civilians perished, with many women and

---

[2]Joe Biden, Speech, The White House, August 22, 2021.

children among the dead. Two hundred additional Afghans were also wounded.

President Biden had a new worst day of his presidency.

Nevertheless, Biden vowed to complete the mission, to complete the evacuation. After the suicide bomb went off, more than 12,000 Americans and Afghans were airlifted out of the country that same day.

On the solemn day of the attack, after Biden spoke of the bravery of the son he lost to brain cancer (who served in Iraq), he called the American soldiers who were killed that day "the backbone of America" and "the best our country has to offer." The empathetic president, monikered by some as "the griever-in-chief," then told the loved ones of the fallen service members this: "We have some sense, like many of you do, of what the families of these heroes were feeling today. You get this feeling that you are being sucked into a black hole in the middle of your chest. There's no way out. My heart aches for you. And I know this. We have a sacred obligation to you that lasts forever."[3]

After offering his patented form of humanity, an obviously shaken, angered Joe Biden made this promise: "To those that carried out this attack, as well as anyone that wishes America harm, we will not forgive. We will not forget. We will hunt you down and make you pay."[4]

Before the weekend was over, Biden's forces preemptively blew up a suspected ISIS-K suicide terrorist's car that was carrying explosives on route to the Hamid Karzei Airport. The American military called the attack imminent.

The day before, Biden had warned of the likelihood of a second attack against Americans and their Afghan allies. Once

---

[3]Joe Biden, Remarks, The White House, August 26, 2021.
[4]Ibid.

again drone assets had been deployed. This time, the U.S. military might have stopped a second terrorist attack before it happened thanks to intelligence assets still in the country; however it was later learned that the U.S. military had killed civilians and not terrorists.

Within three days of the suicide bombing, President Joe Biden and First Lady Jill Biden flew to Dover Base in Delaware to preside over the "dignified transfer" of the 13 fallen soldiers. Eleven of the 13 were younger than 24 years of age—most were very young children when the war began in late 2001. President Biden, surrounded by members of his administration, bowed in prayer as the casket passed by him in the total silence of the gathered.

The media rushed to ask how badly the Biden presidency would be scarred by the chaos associated with the botched Afghanistan pullout. It was the correct question, but it had been asked prematurely. A few of the best journalists and newspapers seemed to understand that.

The *Washington Post* best explained in an op-ed how one should view the president's role in the marred withdrawal: "So Biden owns this, just as Bush owned the accumulated intelligence failures that led to 9/11; just as Jimmy Carter owned the Iranian revolution that was 30 years in the making; just as Gerald Ford owned the last chopper out of Saigon a generation after Harry S. Truman sent the first Americans in."[5]

The author of the op-ed, David Von Drehle, explained the mitigating circumstances in Biden's role: "It is unseemly for veterans of past administrations to fan the flames roasting Biden after failing in their own time to resolve this mess. In their excesses, many are misleading the public as to the situation in Afghanistan when Biden took office—perhaps

[5]David Von Drehle, "Past Presidents Left a Mess in Afghanistan, but Biden Owns the Current Calamity," Op-Ed, *Washington Post*, August 27, 2021.

they don't know it themselves. The country was not secure. The conflict was not stable. The skeleton force of 2,500 remaining U.S. troops was neither safe nor sufficient to repel the Taliban's promised spring offensive."[6]

One decorated retired U.S. general emphasized a different aspect of Biden's role as commander-in-chief: "We have an unusually empathetic president of the United States right now," declared Major General Paul Eaton. "I got to meet with President Biden when he was the vice president, and he is authentic. He wears his heart on his sleeve . . . you get the totality of the man's emotions, and he is 100 percent on board and empathetic with those going through a tough time."[7]

The media coverage of the events in Afghanistan continued and was unsettling and unrelenting. James Fallows, however, a long-time national correspondent for the *Atlantic* and award-winning author, had a different take on the situation. Fallows felt that there were several false equivalents appearing in the media. He said that there were several things a news organization must do in such a chaotic foreign relations situation. One of the media's primary goals, explained Fallows, is "keeping things in perspective. How this [event in Afghanistan] fits in historical terms . . . and I think [this time] it has been a gross failure . . . with the instant equation of the fall of Kabul with the fall of Saigon, which it has almost nothing in [common] except the pictures of helicopters."[8] Fallows pointed out that, for one thing, 30 times the number of American servicepeople were killed in Vietnam as compared with America's longest war in Afghanistan.

....
[6]Ibid.
[7]Paul Eaton, Interview, *Kendis Gibson and Lindsey Reiser Report*, MSNBC, August 29, 2021.
[8]James Fallows, Interviewed by Brian Stelter, *Reliable Sources*, CNN, August 29, 2021.

Don't Abandon Priorities

On Sunday morning, at the end of the weekend of Biden's worst week in office, a category 4 hurricane named *Ida* hit Louisiana hard. It crashed into Louisiana precisely 16 years to the day after *Katrina* leveled New Orleans. President Biden, who earlier presided over the dignified body transference of the 13 slain American soldiers, was later at FEMA, thanking everyone who worked there. Biden was everywhere during the end of this terrible week.

Biden was clearly troubled. He faced three crises simultaneously: Afghanistan; Hurricane *Ida*; and the resurgent Covid-19 Delta variant, fiercer than all previous Covid-19 strains. On the Covid-19 front, because an insufficient number of eligible Americans got vaccinated, there were a million new infections per week likely to kill an additional 100,000 Americans by December 2021.

In the wake of the Afghanistan crisis, all other pressing matters seemed to come to a grinding halt. An international mission gone awry makes implementing domestic policy more challenging. Joe Biden was wounded politically by the Afghan crisis. He badly needed a substantial victory to help right the ship. His eyes moved to the House of Representatives, which returned from their August recess early.

To make sure that his legislative goals would not be neglected, Biden had created a war room in the White House in July to make sure that he was on top of all matters related to infrastructure. According to the *Los Angeles Times*, 20 or so staffers worked on issues related to the two-tier bills: "'The No. 1 priority for our cabinet overall, from our perspective here, is to build support throughout the [August] recess process for the legislative agenda,' explained Neera Tanden, a senior advisor to the president who has overseen the war room since July."[9]

Prior to the Afghan crisis, Biden had been celebrating the fact that his $1.2 trillion "hard infrastructure" bill had been passed by the Senate in sweeping bipartisan fashion, even though it had not been taken up by the House before the August recess. Recall that in the spring of 2021, Biden decided that his best chance to gain passage of his wide-ranging wish list for Americans was to break his infrastructure plan into two separate bills: a smaller hard infrastructure plan (about a $1.2 trillion plan) and a behemoth $3.5 trillion "human infrastructure" plan that addressed healthcare, climate, childcare, education needs, plus much more. Biden and other Democrats did not think that passage of either bill would be the proverbial walk in the park, but the "hard" infrastructure / "human" infrastructure bifurcation made good political sense. For one, it would likely be easier to explain and sell two packages separately to the American people.

Biden knew that he had done a great deal of good in gaining support for his grand vision of a more equitable American financial system, one that could benefit the least wealthy Americans. It was one of the promises of his presidential campaign. Now the future of his most important pieces of legislation was in the hands of lawmakers in Congress. The baton had been passed to Speaker of the House Nancy Pelosi to make positive things happen.

As background, Nancy Pelosi will hold the position of speaker of the House only until 2022. She promised to step down then. Pelosi served twice as House minority leader and speaker. She has led the House Democratic caucus since 2003.

---

[9]Eli Stokols and Noah Bierman, "Biden Focuses on Domestic Agenda, Even as Hot Spots Flare Up Elsewhere," *Los Angeles Times*, August 21, 2021.

Prior to being voted in as speaker for her last time, there was talk that Pelosi's time as speaker was finished. Many in Congress argued that she was a symbol of the past, not the future. Pelosi took on the criticism and the naysayers with her usual brand of dignity and professionalism and was voted as speaker by a narrow margin in early January 2021. As a result of her distinguished performance, perseverance, and ability to keep her caucus united, she will go down in history as one of the most effective speakers in U.S. history.

Joe Biden was smart to rely on Nancy Pelosi. Without her, Biden knew that he would not succeed in passing his infrastructure bills, his top priority. She, however, faced intra-party battles that threatened passage of both bills.

The challenges Pelosi faced in the waning days of August 2021 were considerable. Like in every Congress, different factions tend to vie for vastly different things. In the 117th Congress, Pelosi had a group of moderates that wanted to take the bird in hand, the $1.2 trillion hard infrastructure bill. They demanded an immediate vote on that bill, making the cogent argument that since it had already passed in the Senate, it would surely constitute a big win for the party.

Then there was the left wing of the party, represented by such progressives as Alexandria Ocasio-Cortes and Pramila Jayapal. As the chair for the nearly 100-member Progressive caucus, Jayapal had very strong views on both infrastructure bills.

Progressives decided months earlier that they were far more interested in the larger budget bill. In fact, Ocasio-Cortes said that $3.5 trillion was a small number, and that an eye-popping $10 trillion was needed to help the impoverished, particularly communities of color (few experienced members of Congress felt that figure viable).

Thus, the Progressives wanted both bills joined at the hip, so to speak. Here is how Jayapal explained her caucus position: "As our members have made clear for three months, the two [bills] are integrally tied together, and we will only vote for the [$1.2 trillion] infrastructure bill after passing the [$3.5 trillion] reconciliation bill."[10]

Pelosi's dilemma was plain for all to see. The moderates wanted an immediate one-off vote on the $1.2 trillion bill, and the Progressives refused to vote on the $1.2 trillion plan until they had taken up the $3.5 trillion budget proposal.

It appeared that Speaker Pelosi faced an impossible choice. Her caucus was dug in. Was there no way to break the logjam?

Like she had done many times with flare and dignity, Pelosi did indeed find a temporary stop-gap measure, and she had some help: The White House quietly pressured members of Congress to go along with Pelosi. Ultimately, to gain passage of the $3.5 trillion bill, she promised her caucus a vote on the $1.2 trillion hard infrastructure plan by September 27 (about a month out).

With that promise, things *appeared* to come together only a day after it looked like both bills would fail. The *New York Times* described how events played out: "A divided House approved a $3.5 trillion budget blueprint that would pave the way for a vast expansion of social safety net and climate programs, as Democrats overcame sharp internal rifts to advance a critical piece of President Biden's ambitious domestic agenda. . . . Approving the budget was a major step in Democrats' drive to enact their top priorities—including huge investments in education, childcare, health care, paid leave, and tax increases on wealthy people and corporations—over united Republican opposition. With a single vote on Tuesday, they laid the groundwork to move quickly on legislation that

---

[10]Pramila Jayapal, Press Release, Congressional Progressive Caucus, August 24, 2021.

would accomplish those goals, setting a late September deadline for action on a $1 trillion bipartisan infrastructure package."[11]

After the bill got through the House, Joe Biden extolled: "We are a step closer to truly investing in the American people, positioning our economy for long-term growth, and building an America that out-competes the rest of the world. . . . I also want to thank every Democrat in the House who worked so hard for weeks to reach an agreement. . . . There were differences, strong points of view, they are always welcome. But what is important is that we came together to advance our agenda."[12]

Not so fast. When, on October 1st, President Biden met with the entire Democrat caucus in the bowels of the U.S. Capitol, it was apparent that he was affixing his potential landmark legislation with the progressive wing of his party. They had the numbers, and they had his heart. Biden was not negotiating when he said he wanted both pieces of infrastructure to pass together; nor were the progressives. It was the strength of the Biden-progressives alliance [as well as the will of two moderate senators], that would determine Biden's legislative success or failure.

Put the Planet First

Among Biden's many priorities, climate change is rising. During the 2020 presidential campaign, many Americans felt that Joe Biden did not really care much about the climate. All the noise he was making about it was just a pandering to his left flank, many argued. However, Biden today is attempting to deliver well beyond what he promised during his presidential campaign.

---

[11]Emily Cochrane, "House Passes $3.5 Trillion Budget Plan for Vast Expansion of Safety Net," *New York Times*, August 24, 2021.
[12]Joe Biden, Speech, The White House, August 24, 2021.

As he did on so many issues, he underpromised and over-delivered. After the preceding four years in which climate had been ignored by the previous administration, Biden did not want to let people down. On day one of his presidency, America rejoined the Paris Climate Accords. That sent an important signal to the world.

Biden also elevated climate change to a national security post and created the first climate-related cabinet-level job: the U.S. Special Presidential Envoy for Climate. For that post he appointed former presidential candidate and nominee John Kerry. In addition, Biden directed the federal government to conserve 30 percent of all land and water by 2030.

Biden's decades-long history on climate change is impressive. In 1987, Senator Biden put forward the first real climate bill—the "Global Climate Protection Act." According to *Politifact,* Biden had the longest record on climate change of any of the 2020 presidential candidates.

Here is how *Politifact* described Biden's early work on the environment: "Biden spoke about the bill on the Senate floor in January 1987 in terms that seem uncannily familiar to present-day warnings. He discussed, among other ills, the threat to human habitat resulting from melting polar ice caps and rising sea levels."[13]

The publication *Inside Climate News* explained that the levers of government did not move swiftly in the 1980s. "It was the Global Climate Protection Act of 1986 that was largely put into a spending bill in 1987. The Reagan administration pretty much ignored it, but the bill did call for an EPA national policy on climate change, and annual reports to Congress."[14]

---

[13]John Kruzel, "Was Joe Biden a Climate Change Pioneer in Congress? History Says Yes," *Politifact,* May 8, 2019.
[14]John H. Cushman, Jr., "Debate 2020: The Candidates' Climate Positions & What They've Actually Done," *Inside Climate News,* June 24, 2019.

The author of that piece, John H. Cushman, Jr., analyzed the candidates' records on global warming and climate change. According to Cushman, Biden "had a lifetime environmental voting score of 83 percent from the League of Conservation Voters. In 2007, he supported higher fuel efficiency standards for motor vehicles, which passed, and in 2003, modest caps on greenhouse gas emissions, which didn't."[15]

Regardless of the challenges and opponents to climate change legislation, Biden was undeterred. In 1987, he said, "Life on this planet exists only under highly specialized circumstances. Indeed, so special are these circumstances that even a small rise in temperature could disrupt the entire complicated environment that has nurtured life as we know it."[16]

At the same time, Biden was a central force in encouraging President Reagan to emphasize the policy of climate change in U.S.-Soviet relations. Biden commented, "President Reagan told Secretary General Gorbachev 'that if we had an invasion from Mars, both sides would put aside our differences.' While not an extraterrestrial threat, global warming could prove no less dangerous."[17]

Biden assertions that he was the first lawmaker to introduce a climate change bill have been fact-checked by *Politifact* as true. Biden's lengthy experience helped prepare him to be one of the most forward-thinking presidents in modern history.

Biden took the climate crisis seriously enough to gather 40 of the world's leaders for a Virtual (Zoom) Climate Summit on Earth Day, April 22, 2021. The American leader was pleased that the Chinese dictator Xi Jinping agreed to join the meeting. Biden was not sure he would attend, given that China

---

[15]Ibid.

[16]John Kruzel, "Was Joe Biden a Climate Change Pioneer in Congress? History Says Yes," *Politifact*, May 8, 2020.

[17]Ibid.

contributed just over a quarter of the world's greenhouse gases (the United States is responsible for 13 percent). To illustrate the diversity of people in attendance, consider this: two other individuals in attendance were young activist Greta Thunberg and none other than Pope Francis.

At the Summit, Biden announced: "[The climate crisis] is the existential crisis of our time. . . . Scientists tell us that this is the decisive decade. This is the decade in which we must make decisions that will avoid the worst consequences of the crisis. This is a moral imperative. This is an economic imperative. A moment of peril. But a moment of extraordinary possibilities. Time is short. But I believe we can do this."[18]

"No nation can solve this crisis on their own, as I know you all fully understand," Biden declared. "All of us, all of us, and particularly those of us who represent the world's largest economies, we have to step up. That's why I proposed the huge investment in infrastructure and American innovation. Putting these people to work the United States sets out to cut greenhouse emissions by half by the end of the decade."[19]

Biden's new goal was *twice* as aggressive as the previous target set by the Obama administration. The American president hinged all his remarks on the principle that "inaction is not an option," which was quickly becoming his rallying cry to his fellow citizens and lawmakers.[20]

Nathan Hultman, the director of the University of Maryland's Center on Global Sustainability, explained to the *New York Times* that this would not be an easy task. The *Times* also made it clear that this was an overly ambitious,

[18]Joe Biden, Remarks at the Virtual Leaders Summit on Climate, Opening Session, The White House, April 22, 2021.
[19]Ibid.
[20]Ibid.

unprecedented goal. By the end of the decade, America would have to get half of its energy from renewable sources, such as wind and solar. That is up from 20 percent in the early 2020s.[21] In addition, the United States would need to close its remaining 200 coal plants and fast-forward the development of technology that can ensnare and bury carbon dioxide, rather than letting it seep into the fabric of the atmosphere.

In addition, most cars bought by 2030 would have to be electric, up from a paltry 2 percent in the early 2020s. Electricity would need to replace natural gas in heating all new buildings. Oil and gas companies would need to cut emissions of methane, a gas known for trapping heat, by 60 percent. The country's farming and woodlands would have to be overhauled to remove 20 percent more carbon dioxide from America's air supply.[22]

The *Times* and scores of organizations reported that Biden's colossal $3.5 trillion "human" infrastructure bill package could accomplish a great deal of these goals in combatting climate change. According to the *MIT Technology Review*, "The $3.5 trillion budget plan includes a provision known as the Clean Electricity Payment Program, which would use payments and penalties to encourage utilities to increase the share of electricity they sell from carbon-free sources each year. If it works as hoped, the legislation would ensure that the power sector generates 80% of its electricity from sources like wind, solar, and nuclear plants by 2030, cutting more than a billion tons of annual greenhouse-gas emissions."[23]

[21] Glenn Thrush and Julian E. Barnes, "Biden's Intelligence Director Vows to Put Climate at 'Center' of Foreign Policy," *New York Times*, April 22, 2021; updated May 10, 2021.

[22] Brad Plumer, "Biden Wants to Slash Emissions. Success Would Mean a Very Different America," *New York Times*, April 22, 2021.

[23] James Temple, "The $3.5 Trillion Budget Bill Could Transform the US Power Sector—and Slash Climate Pollution," *MIT Technology Review*, August 23, 2021.

Biden believed that his $3.5 trillion bill would be a first bold step toward putting the planet first and addressing the worst of the climate crisis.

What's the Takeaway?

- **Stick to Reality.** When Biden gave speeches or granted a network interview or a lengthy press conference surrounding a failure, he was duty-bound to look inside himself, apologize first, and then take responsibility. When he failed to do those things, he created a reality gap that the dogged but earnest press corps would not forget.

- **Plan for Every Contingency.** Make plans for worst outcomes. Joe Biden and his administration failed on this metric. They were caught off-guard when the Afghan army collapsed and the Taliban took over in about a dozen days. Despite Biden's insistence that these events could not have been foreseen, many experts disagree. The evacuation could have been planned to take place weeks or months earlier, more quietly.

- **Find Partners for the Biggest, Most Pressing Problems.** Partners can help leaders solve problems. When Biden spoke of the climate crisis, he backed his words with actions. He created a cabinet post for the climate czar, the first president to do so. But when he spoke of not being able to go it alone, he was reaching out to the world's nations to partner with the United States in establishing tough climate regulations.

CHAPTER 6

Focus on Leadership, Not Optics

Madame Speaker, Madame Vice President. . .

No president has ever said those words and it's about time.

—Joe Biden

Heading into Labor Day 2021, President Biden was staring down the barrel of several crises all at once. Hurricane *Ida*, a resurgent Covid-19, and the chaotic exit from Afghanistan were all garnering great media attention. The crisis garnering the most was the marred departure from Afghanistan.

Biden was sharply criticized by most reporters, commentators, Republicans, many Democrats, and allies across the Atlantic and beyond. Yet Biden did not own the war in Afghanistan. Biden had served as president for only 3 percent of the total 20-year war.

In contrast to Biden's critics (including the *Washington Post*'s David Von Drehle, quoted in the previous chapter), world-class author and journalist David Rothkopf of the *Atlantic* explained how he saw the Afghan situation and Biden's role in it: "Joe Biden doesn't 'own' the mayhem on the ground right now. What we're seeing is the culmination of twenty years of bad decisions by U.S. political and military leaders. If anything, Americans should feel proud of what the U.S. government and military have accomplished in these past two weeks. President Biden deserves credit, not blame. . . . [The previous administrations] all conveniently forgot that they were responsible for some of America's biggest errors in this war and instead were incandescently self-righteous in their invective against the Biden administration."[1]

Rothkopf added this important verdict, one that is likely to mirror history's judgment of the war and its evolution: "Unlike his three immediate predecessors in the Oval Office, all of whom also came to see the futility of the Afghan operation, Biden alone had the political courage to fully end America's involvement. Although Donald Trump made a plan to end the war, he set a departure date that fell after the end of his first term and created conditions that made the situation Biden inherited more precarious.[2] And despite significant pressure and obstacles, Biden has overseen a military and government that have managed, since the announcement of America's withdrawal, one of the most extraordinary logistical feats in their recent history."[3]

Retired Major General "Spider" Marks agreed with Rothkopf: "They've achieved an amazing feat of getting over 116,000 Afghan nationals and 6,000 citizens out."[4] One more retired brigadier general weighed in, extolling the enormity of what Biden had accomplished: "We have just been through an extraordinarily rough chapter which closed with us parting Kabul Airfield after twenty years. The president is ruing the loss of our brave service members and brave Afghans. But if you look at just what happened . . . with a clear mission statement, they pulled off an evacuation for the ages."[5]

One day after the last soldier left Afghanistan, Americans heard from the empathetic president in his longest speech

---

[1]David Rothkopf, "Biden Deserves Credit, Not Blame, for Afghanistan," *Atlantic*, August 30, 2021.

[2]After the Afghan evacuation, it was revealed in the book *Peril*, by Bob Woodward and Robert Costa, that Trump had signed a document to end the war on January 15, 2021, while he was still in office.

[3]Rothkopf, 2021.

[4]Interview, *The Lead with Jake Tapper*, CNN, August 30, 2021.

[5]Ibid.

on the topic. President Biden made this forceful, compelling statement: "After twenty years of war in Afghanistan I refuse to send another generation of America's sons and daughters to fight a war that should have ended long ago. To those asking for a third decade of war in Afghanistan I ask: what is the vital national interest?"[6]

President Biden explained to his fellow citizens that the situation in Afghanistan had changed. He raised the issue of mental health to explain the somewhat hidden cost of these long wars: "Eighteen veterans, on average, . . . die by suicide every single day in America, not in a far-off place, but right here in America. There is nothing low-grade or low-risk or low-cost about any war. It's time to end the war in Afghanistan."[7]

That had been Biden's most forceful speech as president against the Afghan war. It was his best speech on the topic because he skillfully laid out his entire approach and thought patterns pertaining to the war.

President Biden was frustrated that the mass evacuation of over 122,000 brave souls did not garner more praise. Pulling off "one of the most extraordinary logistical feats in recent history" was an extraordinary leadership success, which would not have been achieved without help from a talented group of people around him.

Surround Yourself with Talent

When the Biden administration took over the government in January 2021, the federal government was poorly staffed, and the nation was still reeling from Covid-19, the January 6th insurrection, and the Big Lie. According to an aide to Biden,

---

[6]Joe Biden, Remarks, The White House, August 31, 2021.
[7]Ibid.

in early 2021 the machinery and levers of government were in disrepair, and the institution of the White House and entire executive branch were so badly battered that it was akin to an edifice built on quicksand.

Biden needed to bring in a cabinet that reflected his values of transparency, candor, and competence, and he needed to do that quickly. He knew that the team he assembled was critical to rebuilding trust in American government and, more important, American democracy.

Biden selected a cabinet that is 55 percent non-White and 45 percent women. According to *The Hill*, "[U]p and down the administration, women and people of color are taking political roles—in the cabinet, and as political appointees leading Washington's bureaucracies. . . . The Biden administration has seen historic firsts in the form of . . . the first female Treasury secretary, the first Black leader of the Pentagon and the first immigrant to run the Department of Homeland Security."[8]

Biden placed more women in senior roles than any president who preceded him. This included his political director, the head of the domestic policy council, and his legislative affairs director. Added to this already robust and powerful cadre of women are his communications team, its director, press secretary, and deputy press secretary.

However, in perhaps a hundred years from now, President Biden will likely be recognized for one act above all others: the decision in August 2020 to select as his vice presidential running mate Kamala Harris, the first woman and woman of color to serve in the role.

Breaking barriers is a good thing and makes for great optics. But far more important to Biden was Harris's fitness and competence for the highest office. Joe Biden understood that before he selected the California native.

----

[8]Brett Samuels, "Biden's Big Difference? Diversity," *The Hill*, March 3, 2021.

Even though the optics of her selection to the 2020 Democratic ticket were pure magic, her experience and capability were paramount to Biden in his choice. Biden understood that a leader who makes important decisions mostly or solely for optics will almost assuredly fail (think of John McCain's selection of Sarah Palin), but in his choice of Kamala Harris as vice president he did not have this worry.

From 2004 to 2011, Harris served as the hard-charging district attorney of the city of San Francisco and later gained a strong reputation as a crime-fighting attorney general for the State of California until 2017 when she became a senator. In her four years as senator, Harris showed her gravitas as a prosecutor and politician in many ways, perhaps most effectively in the way she peppered nominees and others testifying before the Senate with her tough-as-nails questions.

Politico named her as a leading member of the "Hell-No Caucus" in 2018. She received that distinction for joining other senators like Elizabeth Warren and Bernie Sanders in fighting against Trump's cabinet and other nominations. She voted against picks like Rex Tillerson, Mike Pompeo, and Betsy DeVos, three candidates with questionable qualifications in the Trump administration.

As the junior senator from California, she first announced her run for president on *Good Morning America* in January 2019. She surprised many in December 2019 when she announced her withdrawal from the race, citing lack of funds. Perhaps she sensed it was not her turn to be president, or it is possible she was hoping to be selected as the Democratic vice presidential nominee.

Her reasons for running for president were well-aligned with the goals of Joe Biden. She was interested, not in lofty oratory (although she is an effective public speaker), but in putting more money and equity back into the system to help the poor and forgotten. One of her advisers said she was interested in "big tangible solutions" by increasing teacher's paychecks and implementing child tax credits. She was highly focused on women and women of color.

Once she was Joe Biden's choice for vice president, she felt more comfortable showing off the more empathetic side of herself. Here she spoke in adulatory tones for the great Black women who came before her: "These women picked up the torch and fought on. . . . As Americans, we all stand on their shoulders."[9]

What Harris brought most was a Biden-like devotion and adherence to the laws and institutions that comprise our functioning democracy. She also brought a level of competence, experience, and sharpness of mind that could easily be seen as strengths in a governing partner.

It became clear to Joe Biden that his vice presidential pick would be both historic as well as sagacious. Kamala Harris would bring a great deal to the table—including a substantive inner core that transcended optics.

Make History

Biden's closest aides recognized a new swagger in his step in late April 2021. For the first time in the history of the American experiment, two women sat behind the president as he delivered his State of the Union Address—and not just two women, but one a Black woman of East Asian descent.

It was a striking picture that reminded Americans and people around the globe that the United States is a country in which everything is possible. Joe Biden's first words that night

---

[9]Kamala Harris, Vice Presidential Nomination Acceptance Speech, CNN, August 20, 2020.

ignited much applause from both sides of the aisle. "Madame Speaker, Madame Vice President. . . . No president has ever said those words and it's about time," declared President Biden with a wide smile.[10]

Vice President Kamala Harris sitting next to Speaker of the House Nancy Pelosi was a shining example of the kind of inclusion all leaders should emulate. It is the kind of inclusion that President Biden had campaigned on and the kind he made happen once he was in the Oval Office. That night, he was literally standing in front of history.

Ironically, it took an old White man to widen the aperture of history to break into a boy's club that had persisted since America's founding. Biden cracked several political glass ceilings by selecting Harris, a woman who wears her experience, diversity, and competence naturally and proudly.

Pass the First Leadership Test

Peter Drucker once said, "There is no success without a successor." He also said we often select successors that are "weaker representations of ourselves." Fortunately for him and America, Biden did not make that common mistake when he selected Kamala Harris to be his vice president.

When you are president of the United States, choosing a successor is not only the first key management decision; it is also likely to be one of the most important. This decision is magnified when you are the oldest president ever elected to the office. While the median age of an incoming president is 55, Joe Biden will celebrate his 80th birthday right after the mid-terms of 2022.

---

[10]Joe Biden, State of the Union Address, The White House, April 29, 2021.

Selecting a successor grows in importance as the responsibility and complexity of the position expands. Long before taking the oath of office, Joe Biden passed his first leadership test: *choosing a competent successor*. Unlike the succession plans required for less important jobs, the succession plan for the highest job in the land must be in place months before the "candidate" starts the job. For Biden, work as president started at noon on January 20, 2021, but for Joe Biden the candidate, work began long before he announced his succession plan on August 11, 2020. That was, of course, the day he selected Kamala Harris to serve as his vice president and possible successor. His decision did not come lightly, but given the incredible strengths of Kamala Harris, it was the right one.

Of course, human beings are not optics, but for better or worse, perceptions are changed by the people a leader chooses to implement his or her stated agenda. Biden's rainbow cabinet, led by more women than men, and his vice president said a great deal about the promises kept by the man who sat behind the Resolute desk in the Oval Office.

What's the Takeaway?

- **Don't Punt Urgent Decisions.** Do not delay or put off important decisions regarding urgent matters. The Afghan evacuation crisis makes this all too clear. The most important decisions made by managers are almost always people decisions.

- **Hire Those Who Share Your Values.** Joe Biden hired people who were eminently qualified for their respective positions. As important, they shared his vision and values. Biden created a cabinet that was diverse, inclusive, transparent, and honest.

- **Create a Succession Plan.** All leaders and managers must plan for their own departures from their current positions. Succession plans are essential for the continuity of every organization.

CHAPTER 7

Build a Legacy

Failure at some point in your life is inevitable, but giving up is unforgivable.

—Joe Biden

T he day before his first Memorial Day weekend as president, President Joe Biden declared, "Covid cases are down [close to 90 percent from the highs of the winter of 2020], Covid deaths are down, unemployment filings are down, hunger is down. Vaccinations are up, jobs are up. Growth is up. To put it simply, America is back. America is on the move."[1] Biden had much to celebrate that day.

Little did he know that the world was about to be turned upside down once again. By the time Labor Day arrived, the United States had experienced a terrible reversal of Covid-19 fortune. That was particularly true in the most Southern states. Daily cases had been up since July 4, due to the Delta variant, a far more virulent form of the strain. Millions of Americans, spurred on by lawmakers and governors who politicized science, had enough of the virus. But no matter how "finished" people were with the virus, this new, more deadly Delta variant was nowhere finished with America.

Biden was understandably frustrated. He and his administration could not have done more to make multiple vaccines (Pfizer, Moderna, and J&J) free and available within five miles of most every American's home. Yet vaccine hesitancy was literally killing America.

----

[1]Joe Biden, Remarks, The White House May 27, 2021.

While most Americans were accustomed to choosing a political party, they were less familiar with the way Covid-19 was used as some oath barometer of Republican party allegiance. Some GOP governors, for example, banned mask mandates even though masks save lives (e.g., Florida's Ron DeSantis and Texas's Greg Abbott).

Post-2017, it is not difficult to imagine how science and vaccines became the key political football of the early 2020s. It became apparent after Trump's second impeachment acquittal and the violent insurrection of January 6, 2021, that most Republican lawmakers were still praying at the altar of Trump. Only 46 percent of Republican Trump supporters were vaccinated, compared with nearly 90 percent of Democrats. Red states, mostly in the South, had the worst Covid-19 vaccination rates.

Those who refused to get vaccinated were not only putting themselves at great risk, but they also provided hosts for the powerful, highly transmissible Delta variant. As a result, where the unvaccinated lived, hospitalization records were broken. Just about 100 percent (95 percent) of the hospitalized were unvaccinated. This occurred as the United States entered its fall and winter months.

By September 1, 2021, working with local and state governments, the United States had administered 375 million doses, and the number of shots was expected to top 400 million by early 2022.[2] However, despite the "wartime footing," only 54 percent of Americans were fully vaccinated.

It wasn't as if these events were unforeseeable. At the beginning of his presidency, *Time* magazine ran a cover story on President Biden and articulated his nearly impossible challenge: "Biden now leads a country divided between

---

[2]Worldwide, more than 5.5 *billion* doses had been administered.

Americans who believe in facts and Americans who distrust them, between those who want a multiracial Republic and those who seek to invalidate nonwhite votes, between those with faith in democratic institutions and those who put faith only in Trump."[3]

Be Pragmatic and Bold

Joe Biden's domestic agenda was more progressive than fellow Democrats expected. Even the Bernie Sanders/Elizabeth Warren wing of the party expressed their approval over the sheer size and depth of the first three Biden bills.

Biden's $1.9 trillion Covid-19 package had the greatest effect on mitigating poverty and redistributing wealth than any other plan or bill since the 1960s. This relief package was enormous enough to last for months and years before the sum would be spent. It gave a needed jolt to the economy and much needed help for families who did not have the means to move past the crisis. The breadth of the package also afforded Biden the time he needed to set the table for subsequent large bills.

Biden then pushed further with his two infrastructure bills, totally almost $5 trillion. He reached mightily with these proposed huge bills, but only when he thought he had a good chance of success. He combined boldness with a pragmatic undergirding. He took risks, but only after mentally weighing the odds and determining that he had some chance of success. Biden knew that for as long as he controlled both chambers of Congress, even by the slimmest of margins, his landmark legislation stood at least a chance of passage.

---

[3]Charlotte Alter, "How Joe Biden Handles a Divided America Will Define His Legacy," *Time*, January 21, 2021.

Biden's boldness in pushing the envelope no doubt arose from his belief that, since two of the last three presidents were Republican, it was high time that an American leader took care of the people the GOP often ignored, such as the poor and people of color.

Biden's multi-trillion-dollar domestic bills earned him a comparison in the press to two notable twentieth-century presidents with completely different personas: the 32nd president, Franklin D. Roosevelt, and the 36th president, Lyndon B. Johnson.

The president of the LBJ Foundation, Mark Updegrove, voiced this interesting conclusion: "As a candidate, Biden preferred to talk about the New Deal. But if you look at what Biden might be able to achieve, it equates more to LBJ."[4]

Much like Johnson, Biden was trying to level the playing field by passing huge bills that would create middle-class jobs and help the poor. Johnson also was both pragmatic and bold. He was the man responsible for the sweeping programs that became known as "The Great Society," which included three key civil rights bills and Medicare. If Biden were able to secure passage of all of his infrastructure bills, he too would be remembered as transformational.[5]

Consider Your Legacy

Six weeks into his first term, President Biden held a secret meeting with presidential historians to discuss his legacy.

[4]Ron Elving, "Can Biden Join FDR And LBJ In The Democratic Party's Pantheon?" NPR, April 17, 2021.

[5]In assessing presidential legacy, however, it is accomplishments as well as defeats that count. Unfortunately for Johnson, the Vietnam War overshadowed much of his domestic accomplishments. Whether the debacle in Afghanistan permanently overshadows Biden's successes remains to be seen.

Three of the most important historical referees of the modern era were in attendance. Biden had entrusted historian and sometime adviser/speechwriter Jon Meacham to arrange the meeting, which included well-known historians Doris Kearns Goodwin and Michael Beschloss.

When Washington watchers learned of the "How Do I Create a Legacy" meeting, a great many were surprised. That sort of meeting might be expected in the last year of a presidency, not in the first. But Biden was aiming at being a great president and welcomed the views of top historians. He wanted to be a legacy-making president who would make a real difference in people's lives.

Biden no doubt enjoyed his discussion among the best of the best historians. Biden loved the aroma of history, something he had in common with other great presidents. They had a burning desire in their guts to help people with the time and power they had while serving as president. The best presidents knew what they wanted to achieve. Or they figured it out once in office. They understood how political chessboards could be turned over in an instant. The best also had humility and empathy.

Return to Empathy

Joe Biden's avuncular manner and speaking style were much closer to FDR's soothing style than LBJ's. Both Biden and Roosevelt found a way to talk to the American people in a way that let them know they had an authentic, empathetic leader who cared about *them*.

Franklin Roosevelt held office from 1933 to 1945, the longest presidential tenure in American history. In his twelve years, he accomplished more than any president since

Abraham Lincoln. "Of course, some of this was the product of circumstances; the Great Depression and the rise of Germany and Japan were beyond FDR's control. But his responses to the challenges he faced made him a defining figure in American history," said William Leuchtenburg, the William Rand Kenan Jr. professor emeritus of history at the University of North Carolina at Chapel Hill.[6]

Roosevelt communicated beautifully with the American people through his fireside radio chats. When he became president, radio was considered a new, ultramodern medium. Within a week of his first chat, the number of mail workers in the White House catapulted from 1 to 70 to deal with 500,000 thank you letters that poured into Washington, D.C., to thank the president for his soothing voice on the other end of the radio.

FDR's presidency spanned several remarkable events, two of which bookended his presidency. The first was the Great Depression, which continued to wreak great havoc on the American economy throughout the 1930s. The second event was World War II. America needed an empathizer-in-chief and they had one.

Roosevelt was one of America's most empathetic leaders. He was stricken with polio 12 years before he became president. According to historian Doris Kearns Goodwin, it was the crippling disease that gave him a new appreciation and understanding of other Americans. "He reached out to know them, to understand them, to pick up their emotions, to put himself into their shoes. . . . He came to empathize with the poor and the underprivileged, with people to whom fate had dealt a difficult hand."[7]

---

[6]William Leuchtenburg, "Franklin D. Roosevelt: Impact and Legacy," millercenter .org, n.d. Accessed September 12, 2021.

[7]"Character Above All," Excerpted from an Essay by Doris Kearns Goodwin, pbs.org, n.d. Accessed September 12, 2021.

Publications like *U.S. News & World Report* lauded Roosevelt's "ability to empathize with his fellow citizens, to show that he cared for them and would do everything he could to help them, as one of his most important attributes as president."[8] And the *HuffPost* explained that Roosevelt was "a man who knew and felt pain every day as a result of his polio."[9] He appreciated Americans' pain.[10]

Like Roosevelt, Joe Biden suffered pain throughout his life. He too channeled that pain into becoming the extremely empathetic leader he is today.

Be a Steady Hand

Biden won the 2020 election because Americans thought he would do better than Trump in dealing with Covid-19. The citizens of the United States responded to the calamity of the previous four years by voting in a steady hand and the most empathetic president in at least a generation.

In a real sense, Biden was dealt an awful hand. No amount of empathy could erase what America and the world watched over the previous half a dozen years. Our adversaries had learned how to exploit a nation split down the middle.

In 1858, Abraham Lincoln delivered the "House Divided" speech after being nominated to the state senate in Springfield. In doing so, he quoted scripture: "Every kingdom divided against itself is brought to desolation; and every city or house divided against itself shall not stand."[11]

[8]Kenneth T. Walsh, "FDR: The President Who Made America into a Superpower," *U.S. News & World Report*, April 10, 2015.

[9]Frank Well, "Working with Roosevelt," *HuffPost*, January 5, 2012.

[10]The information in Notes 7, 8, and 9 comes from Jess Bolluyt, *Cheatsheet*, April 3, 2018.

[11]Gospel of Matthew 12:25, King James version.

The America inherited by Biden was the opposite of united. "Faced with such rampant and cynical senselessness," said Charlotte Alter in *Time*, "[t]he word unity seems to have lost its meaning. House Republicans pleaded for 'unity' as they voted against impeaching Trump; to them, unity meant something closer to political impunity. When Biden calls for unity, he envisions bipartisan collaboration, a kind of peace through process."[12]

Biden was clear in how he intended to get things done. With a half-century of experience in politics, Biden knew that effective governance depended on a certain rhythm or cadence, like a conductor's interpretation of a musical score. His cadence was to move quickly and steadily to set things back on solid ground and with hope reunify the nation.

After four chaotic years in which America's standing in the world had been badly diminished, the United States was suddenly "back." U.S. allies had watched hopelessly when the people of the United States elected Donald Trump in 2016. With the election of Biden, the nation had a leader again who was respected both inside its borders and on foreign shores.

What's the Takeaway?

- **Go for Greatness.** Leaders should think big and not limit their sights. Joe Biden started out with the idea of showing Americans that government can get big things accomplished for all Americans. He set out to do that time and again, starting with nearly 400 million Covid-19 vaccination shots in arms and dealing with the financial aftermath of the pandemic.

[12]Charlotte Alter, "How Joe Biden Handles a Divided America Will Define His Legacy," *Time*, January 21, 2021.

- **Never Forget the First Priority.** Forgetting your first priority can lead to trouble. Biden came into office with Covid-19 at the top of his priority list. Unfortunately for him and the American people, just when it looked as if things were getting back to normal, the Delta variant became dominant and deadly.

- **Build Bridges, not Walls.** Biden was staking his presidency on his ability to unite a fractious Democrat party. President Biden was betting on Mr. Franklin's famous edict: "We must, indeed, all hang together or, most assuredly, we shall all hang separately."

Acknowledgments

I would like to first offer my warm thanks to the A-team at John Wiley.

I thank Shannon Vargo for her sagacity and vision, as well as her thoughts on what *not* to include in the book. Along with Shannon, I thank my former colleague Richard Narramore, one of the most tenured acquisition editors in publishing. Also, my thanks to Deborah Schindlar for keeping the trains running on time. Victoria Anllo helped maintain strong communication between publisher and author.

I also want to thank the Krames family's very own "Discord" team. This impressive group includes Dylan (*Oddball*), Dean (*Mobile*), and Kevin (*Mrs. Kwan*). It was this reclusive panel who helped me to select the perfect computer for this assignment. I look forward to sharing a post-Covid chicken dinner with these estimable individuals.

I thank Dr. Mark Walker for his singular insights on the 10,000-hour rule. That afforded me an additional perspective on the Anders Ericsson research and the two books it sparked. I also thank Dr. Birnbaum and William Goodfriend for living up to their names and the legacy of the Dutch Quadrangle.

I also offer my thanks to the two young men who provided the inspiration I needed to get out of bed each morning for my 4 a.m. writing sessions.

Noah Krames helped keep me on a tight time track. He drew his red line in the sand with a briefer subtitle—and he got his way!

Joshua Krames garners a special acknowledgment here for his political acumen, his commonsense insights, and his ability to learn and help pen the book's notes. Two years before being asked for his first college essay, he proved himself as a great sounding board with first-rate publishing instincts.

A final thought on Joshua, Noah, and the Discord group. Thanks to them and the futures they envision, the United States will execute on the one critical issue confronting us all: our endangered environment. They have the passion, understand technology, and are passionate about this cause above all others. Godspeed to them all.

About the Author

Jeffrey A. Krames is a leadership expert and has spent four decades in business book publishing. He is the author of nine leadership books, several of which were national and international bestsellers. Krames is the former vice president and head of the business book division of McGraw-Hill and is the former editor-in-chief of Portfolio. He has appeared on CNN, CNN International, Fox News, CNBC, BBC, PBS, MSNBC, Fox, Fox Business, CBS, NBC, and more. His work and opinion pieces have been published in the *New York Times, Newsweek, BusinessWeek, Time Magazine,* the *Wall Street Journal,* the *Chicago Tribune,* the *L.A. Times,* and many more newspapers in the United States, Asia, South America, and Europe.

Index